Oilcloth
Inspirations

A DAVID & CHARLES BOOK

Copyright © Dessain et Tolra / Larousse, 2007

Originally published in France as *Toile Cirée*

First published in the UK in 2008 by David & Charles Ltd

David & Charles is an F+W Publications Inc. company
4700 East Galbraith Road
Cincinnati, OH 45236

A catalogue record for this book is available from the British Library.

ISBN-13: 978-0-7153-2965-8 paperback
ISBN-10: 0-7153-2965-0 paperback

Printed in China by SNP
for David & Charles
Brunel House, Newton Abbot, Devon

For David & Charles
Assistant Editor: Sarah Wedlake
Art Editor: Sarah Clark
Designer: Joanna Ley
Production Controller: Beverley Richardson
Visit our website at www.davidandcharles.co.uk

David & Charles books are available from all good bookshops;
alternatively you can contact our Orderline on 0870 9908222 or
write to us at FREEPOST EX2 110, D&C Direct, Newton Abbot, TQ12 4ZZ
(no stamp required UK only); US customers call 800-289-0963 and
Canadian customers call 800-840-5220.

Oilcloth
Inspirations

SOPHIE BESTER

WITH PHOTOGRAPHS BY
FABRICE BESSE

David and Charles

WWW.MYCRAFTIVITY.COM

To three women I love dearly
My grandmother, my mother, and my daughter

Many thanks also to my husband
for his help and his limitless patience!

I would like to thank the following for the loan of materials and items
for the designs and the photo shoots:

Laura Ashley, Bohin, Chehoma, Comptoir de Famille, DMC, Hervé Gambs, Jacadi,
Le Jacquard Français, Kenzo Maison (Arc International), Cath Kidston, Lefranc-Bourgeois,
Loisirs et Création, Luminarc, Maped, Véronique Miss, Moline, Plastique, Les 3 Suisses,
Truffaut and Villeroy & Boch.

Thanks also to Valérie Côme, Mélanie Voituriez, Judith, Iris and Mina Dessons-Ben Ichou,
Marie Hélène Deguilhem and Isabelle Leloup for their invaluable assistance and their
warm reception at the photo shoots.

FOREWORD

As is often the case with these things, it all began when I was a child. It started with a stain: a nasty-looking stain – I forget now whether it was ice cream or orangeade – the first time my grandparents took me out to a restaurant. And so it was with great apprehension that I awaited the ruling of my darling grandmother, who had schooled us in the art of 'no-crumbs' dining. 'Don't worry, dear,' came the response, 'it's oilcloth.' My mishap vanished as if by magic beneath a paper napkin. I was off the hook, but the mystery of the tablecloth still eluded me.

As time went by I forgot about the tablecloth, until my daughter was a toddler who loved to mess about with anything she could get her hands on and thought it would be a fantastic idea to paint directly on to the table. Inspiration came from my mother, who finds the poetic side of every situation and advised me to get hold of some oilcloth. Unable to overcome my 1960s prejudices, I replied 'Great idea!', hiding my true feelings about how awful I imagined it would be.

All the same, I went along to a store and was an instant convert. I loved them all as soon as I set eyes on them: retro kitsch, old-fashioned designs from my childhood, stunning designer prints and traditional English country-style fabrics, all of them beautiful, sparkling and bright.

And, without my even realizing, this book had already begun.

Sophie Bester

CONTENTS

THE GREAT OUTDOORS

VINTAGE CHIC

SUMMER ESSENTIALS

Oilcloth
or coated fabrics?

OILCLOTH

There are many different types of oilcloth.

Thin oilcloth is very inexpensive but is more often than not of mediocre quality: do not expect it to last long or be hard-wearing. It also has a tendency to crack but is easy to work with because it is very supple. Even so, it would be very unwise to make the cheap and cheerful shopper of your dreams from this type of oilcloth: you'll be lucky if it lasts more than a couple of days! I have unearthed incredible fabrics, mainly patterned, in local hardware stores. Hidden away inside these shops you can sometimes find amazing pieces at rock-bottom prices, so have a good rummage around. This is where you're most likely to find lace effect oilcloth, too. These types of oilcloth are perfect for quite small projects and objects that don't need to be too hard-wearing.

Specialist stores and some screen printers, on the other hand, sell very strong thick and semi-thick oilcloth in such a wide variety of patterns that I often find myself wanting to buy the whole shop! This oilcloth is incredibly hard-wearing and very easy to clean, and its glossy coating keeps its shine even when wiped time and time again. The cotton backing means it can be pressed with a cool iron. For designs that must be made to last and will get the most wear, like large bags, pouffes or chair seats, you should be prepared to pay a little more.

COATED FABRIC

As their name suggests, coated fabrics are lengths of cotton or linen which have been coated through various different processes.

PVC-coated fabrics have a satin-like or glossy finish. What the fabric loses in terms of suppleness in the coating process it gains in strength and is therefore perfectly suited to kitchen use.

Acrylic-coated fabrics look very different and have a matte finish. The coating on these fabrics is practically invisible and barely palpable. The fabric remains unbelievably supple, allowing you to make pleats, flowers and frills. These types of coated fabric are perfect for dining room tablecloths because they drape just like normal fabric. Although stains are easily removed, the fabrics are more fragile. Wine spillages and sticky or greasy stains should be wiped off immediately.

Ironing

You can iron the reverse of thick or thin oilcloths. The iron should be cool with the steam setting off. Place a clean white cotton cloth between the iron and the oilcloth. On contact with the heat the fabric will soften; wait until it has cooled completely before working with it.

Coated fabrics can be pressed on the reverse using a hotter iron on the steam setting.

Cleaning

An absolute joy! As a waterproof fabric, oilcloth makes light work of wine spills and chocolate stains made by young and old alike. A sponge and a little washing-up liquid are all it takes to keep them looking their best. Their colours are fade-resistant and not even the stickiest of blackcurrant jams will wear down that shine!

Gluing

Glues can be the bearers of surprises – and not always nice ones, so choose your glue very carefully. Always test the glue on a small fabric swatch, set aside for a few days and check to see if there are any air bubbles, blisters or other evils that will ruin your design.

Recommending that you purchase solvent-free superglues is simply not enough. When used on oilcloth, some glues have truly unsightly chemical reactions and it is impossible, given how many different types of glue and qualities of oilcloth there are, to know in advance what the result will be and to apply any kind of rule. I had very few problems when making the designs in this book, but on the basis of the rare disasters I have had in the past I would urge you to test each glue and oilcloth combination before getting started.

Sewing

SEWING BY HAND

Thin oilcloth is relatively easy to sew using a large needle with a pointed tip. Sewing thick oilcloth by hand, however, is a much more strenuous affair! Use a leather needle with a triangular point which will pass through the fabric with ease and wear a thimble to protect the tip of your finger. Remember that when sewing both types of oilcloth there is no room for error, in particular when working with plain fabrics. Any hole made by a needle is permanent and cannot be undone! Take care not to mess up your sewing and avoid having to start over again on a new piece of fabric. Do not pin your work too close to the design: always pin at least 5mm ('/₄in) from the cutting line. Marks are somewhat less conspicuous on coated fabrics.

TIP

When sewing together two pieces of oilcloth you will find they have a tendency to slide around. Use small clothes pegs to help keep the two pieces together and remove them as you sew. This is particularly important for circles.

MACHINE SEWING

The golden rule is to be gentle on the foot pedal of the machine. A presser foot has an unfortunate tendency to stick to oilcloth, particularly when sewing on the right side of the fabric. Work with the machine by pulling gently on the fabric. Take the time to mark the seams with a fabric pencil or fabric pen when working on the wrong side of the oilcloth. This is essential for keeping your sewing on course and preventing what I call 'drunken stitching', which is not always easy when your machine is making no headway and then suddenly goes off like a shot!

If you find that your oilcloth sticks to the machine too much, insert a sheet of tissue paper between the oilcloth and the machine foot. This is an effective but time-consuming solution because it requires you to painstakingly remove the tissue paper from your work afterwards. I use this method only as a last resort.

Stitches

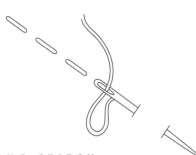

RUNNING STITCH

Running stitch is the easiest stitch for attaching two pieces of fabric together or outlining a motif. The smaller and closer together the stitches, the more secure they will be. At the other end of the scale, long, tacking-style stitches will give less secure results.

Your stitches should be evenly spaced and the same length as the spaces between them.

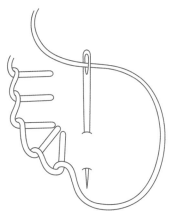

BLANKET STITCH

Blanket stitch is used principally to form edges that stop your fabric from fraying and getting damaged. It is also used to sew two pieces of fabric together and gives a more attractive finish than running stitch and backstitch. Space your stitches out according to the effect you want.
Sew a slanted stitch to turn corners.

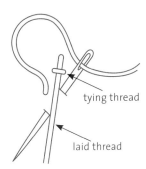

tying thread

laid thread

COUCHING

This stitch is one of a range of couching stitches. In this technique, a thread is laid along your fabric – the laid thread – and then secured with small stitches using another thread known as the tying thread. This stitch allows you to work with different colours and/or materials. You could use pink perle cotton for your laid thread and violet stranded cotton for your tying thread, for example.

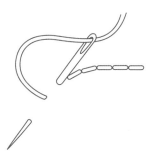

BACKSTITCH

This stitch is very secure and can be used instead of a machine stitch because it forms a continuous line along your fabric. It requires a little more practice than running stitch, especially on thick fabrics like oilcloth.
To keep your stitches even, avoid making them too long.

THE GREAT OUTDOORS

Princess wellingtons

MATERIALS REQUIRED

(for child's wellington boots size 28–30)

- Pair soft wellington boots in pink
- 50cm (20in) transparent oilcloth with violet daisy print
- 20 x 40cm (8 x 16in) thick oilcloth in pink with white polka dots
- 14 purple sequin flowers
- 14 white self-adhesive Velcro circles 1cm ($^1/_2$in) in diameter
- Fine leather needle with triangular point
- Nylon thread 2.5mm thick
- All-purpose gel glue
- Soft pencil
- Tracing paper
- Ruler
- All-purpose scissors

1. PREPARATION

Enlarge the scalloped motif by 170 per cent. Copy it on to tracing paper and cut out. Lay the strip of pink oilcloth wrong side up and draw two rectangles 9 x 38cm ($3^1/_2$ x 15in) in pencil. These dimensions are for the boots on which the design is based. The depth of the scalloped motif, 9cm ($3^1/_2$in), will be the same for any pair of boots but its circumference may vary. To work out the circumference, measure around the top of your boots and add 4cm ($1^5/_8$in).

2. MAKING SCALLOPED STRIPS

Place the scalloped motif template on one of the oilcloth rectangles. Copy the outline, moving the template along as you go to give you a scalloped strip measuring 7.5 x 38cm (3 x 15in). Repeat on the second rectangle. Cut out the two strips.

3. MAKING THE FLOWERS

Cut out 14 flowers from the daisy print oilcloth. Resize them if necessary, trimming the petals until you have flowers measuring 4–4.5cm ($1^5/_8$–$1^3/_4$in) in diameter.

4. ASSEMBLY

Fit one of the strips around the top of one boot. At the back of the boot make two marks on the right side where the scalloping overlaps. Take off the strip and sew the ends together on the reverse with a backstitch (see page 15). Trim the excess. Repeat this process on the second boot. Place the strips back on the boots. Make four marks 3cm ($1^1/_4$in) from the top of each boot and attach the strips with three small stitches at each of these points. Knot the thread after each set of stitches.

5. DECORATING THE STRIPS

Glue a sequin flower into the centre of each daisy. Leave to dry. Stick the loop side of the Velcro circles on the backs of the daisies, in the centre. Stick the hook side on to the boots 3cm ($1^1/_4$in) from the top, spreading them out evenly (seven flowers per boot). Press the flowers on to the circles.

Flower coasters

1. CUTTING OUT THE MOTIFS

Photocopy the flower template. Copy on to tracing paper and cut out. Cut one 18cm (7¹/₈in) square in the thin oilcloth and another in the thick oilcloth.

Lay the thin oilcloth square on a table with the tracing paper flower template on top, and the square of thick oilcloth on top of that. Pin the two oilcloth squares together at 2cm (⁷/₈in) intervals, 1.5cm (³/₄in) outside the tracing paper. Do not pin the tracing paper. Cut the two oilcloths along the outline of the tracing paper.

2. ADDING THE SMALL FLOWERS

Using a leather needle and sewing thread, sew the eight silk flowers to the thin oilcloth flower with a few stitches. Refer to the template as a guide for positioning. When you have sewn on all the flowers, place the thick oilcloth flower on top of the flower you have decorated. Adjust the two flowers so they sit exactly one on top of the other. Trim a little off a petal if necessary. When the two flowers fit perfectly together, hold them in place with a small clothes peg on each petal.

3. ASSEMBLY

Thread a chenille needle with perle cotton to match the colour of the silk flowers. Ensure that you have enough thread to sew a blanket stitch (see page 15) all the way around. The two layers of oilcloth may slide around as you sew; remove the clothes pegs as you go and smooth the two layers out frequently to avoid creases.

MATERIALS REQUIRED

(to make three coasters)

- 54 x 18cm (21¹/₄ x 7⁷/₈in) thick transparent oilcloth
- 54 x 18cm (21¹/₄ x 7⁷/₈in) thin transparent oilcloth
- 8 silk flowers 2.5cm (1in) in diameter in three colours
- Chenille needle
- Fine leather needle with triangular point
- Sewing thread to match the flowers
- Perle cotton to match the flowers
- Pins
- 6 small clothes pegs
- Pencil
- Tracing paper
- All-purpose scissors

Mini armchair

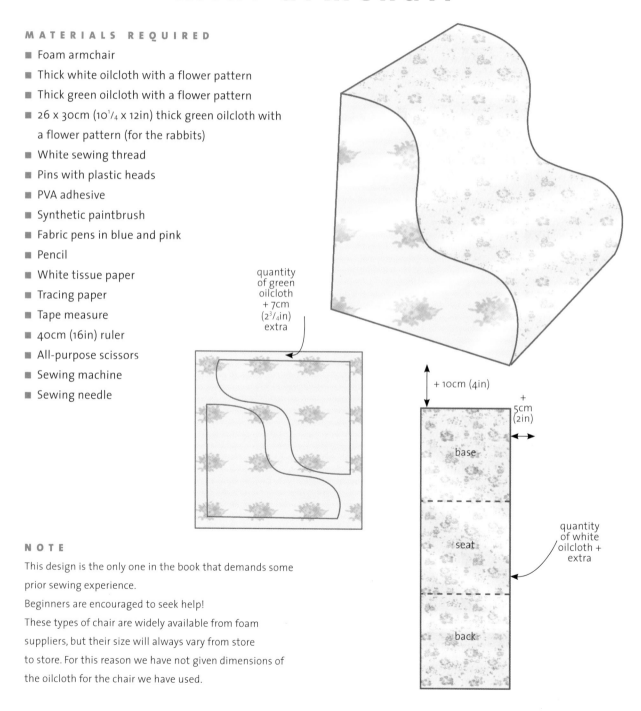

MATERIALS REQUIRED

- Foam armchair
- Thick white oilcloth with a flower pattern
- Thick green oilcloth with a flower pattern
- 26 x 30cm (10$\frac{1}{4}$ x 12in) thick green oilcloth with a flower pattern (for the rabbits)
- White sewing thread
- Pins with plastic heads
- PVA adhesive
- Synthetic paintbrush
- Fabric pens in blue and pink
- Pencil
- White tissue paper
- Tracing paper
- Tape measure
- 40cm (16in) ruler
- All-purpose scissors
- Sewing machine
- Sewing needle

quantity of green oilcloth + 7cm (2$\frac{3}{4}$in) extra

+ 10cm (4in)

+ 5cm (2in)

base

seat

back

quantity of white oilcloth + extra

NOTE

This design is the only one in the book that demands some prior sewing experience.

Beginners are encouraged to seek help!

These types of chair are widely available from foam suppliers, but their size will always vary from store to store. For this reason we have not given dimensions of the oilcloth for the chair we have used.

1. MAKING THE PATTERNS FOR THE CHAIR

Place the tissue paper on one of the sides of the armchair and trace the outline carefully with a pencil. Cut it out. Do the same on the other side of the chair. Lay the two templates out flat, fitting them together to form a square. Measure the square and add 7cm (2³/₄in) to your measurements. This will tell you how much green oilcloth you need to buy. Use a tape measure to measure round the armchair starting at the bottom of the back up to the top, over the curved back and seat and along the base. Add up the measurements for the back, seat and base. Add at least 10cm (4in) to the total length and 5cm (2in) to the width. This will tell you how much white oilcloth you will need.

2. CUTTING OUT THE SIDES

Cut out the pattern for one of the sides along the lines. Lay it on the back of the green oilcloth. Draw around the outline in a blue fabric pen. Using the pink fabric pen, go around the outline again, this time 1.5cm (³/₄in) further away. Repeat for the other side. Cut out the two side pieces along the pink outlines.

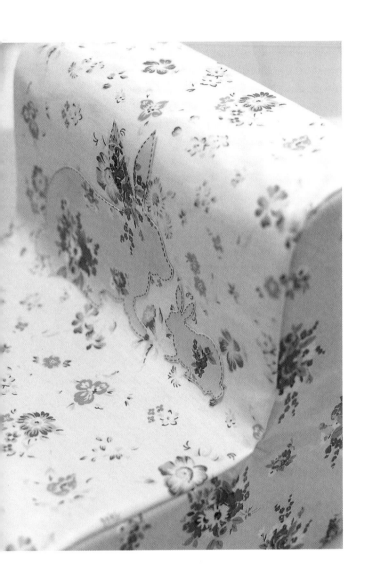

4. PUTTING THE COVER TOGETHER

This is the trickiest stage and the success of your armchair cover will depend on your pinning, which must be perfect. The most important thing is to take your time. Lay the white oilcloth right side up. Take one of the green side pieces and pin it to the white strip, right sides together, starting at the bottom of the back and ensuring that the blue lines match perfectly. Insert pins all round very close together and keep checking to see that the blue lines are still matching. Make sure the fabric is evenly distributed round the curved sections. Machine-sew all round along the blue line. Take out the pins and repeat with the other side piece. Turn the cover to the right side and try it on the foam chair for size. Remove the foam chair and trim the excess from the ends and along the seams, 3mm ($^1/_8$in) from the edge. Put the cover on to the chair and oversew the opening along the base with small stitches using a needle and white thread.

5. FINISHING TOUCHES

Enlarge the two rabbit templates by 30 per cent. Copy on to tracing paper. Transfer the outlines on to the reverse of the green oilcloth. Make sure you copy the rabbits the right way round so they face each other. Using a paintbrush, coat the back of each rabbit with PVA adhesive. Stick them on to the back of the chair, using the photo as a guide. Smooth them over gently to remove air bubbles.

3. CUTTING OUT THE MIDDLE SECTION

Lay the white oilcloth flat on a table, wrong side up. Using a blue fabric pen and a ruler, draw a rectangle exactly the same size as the measurements for the back, seat and base sections. With the pink fabric pen, draw a second outline 1.5cm ($^3/_4$in) further out along each long edge and 5cm (2in) further out along each short edge. Cut this rectangle out along the pink line.

Butterfly doilies

MATERIALS REQUIRED

(to make one doily)

- 35cm (13³/₄in) square of thick transparent oilcloth
- 35cm (13³/₄in) square of transparent oilcloth with a butterfly print
- Paper doily 26cm (10¹/₄in) in diameter in a pastel colourway
- Fine leather needle with triangular point
- Invisible polyamide thread
- Pins
- 8 small clothes pegs
- Pencil
- A3 sheet of tracing paper
- Ruler
- All-purpose scissors
- Iron
- White cotton cloth

1. PREPARATION

Place the tracing paper on the doily and copy its outline adding an extra 5mm (¹/₄in). Cut it out. Iron the two oilcloth squares, placing a clean cloth between the iron and the oilcloth and with the iron on the cotton setting. Leave each square to cool for 15 minutes.

Lay the square of transparent oilcloth on a table with the tracing paper template on top and the square of butterfly print oilcloth right side up on top of that. Pin the two oilcloth squares together at 2cm (⁷/₈in) intervals 2.5cm (in) from the tracing paper. Do not pin the tracing paper.

2. CUTTING OUT THE DOILY

Cut the shape out carefully around the outside of the tracing paper. As you work, hold the cut sections together with small clothes pegs. When you have finished cutting, gently lift half of the butterfly oilcloth, take out the template and replace it with the paper doily. Ensure that it is perfectly centred and hold the three layers together with small clothes pegs all around the outside.

3. SEWING THE DOILY

Using a fine leather needle and polyamide thread, sew the two oilcloth layers together with a backstitch (see page 15). Remove the clothes pegs as you go to prevent the two pieces of oilcloth sliding around on top of each other and creasing.

To prevent creasing, smooth out the two pieces of oilcloth at regular intervals.

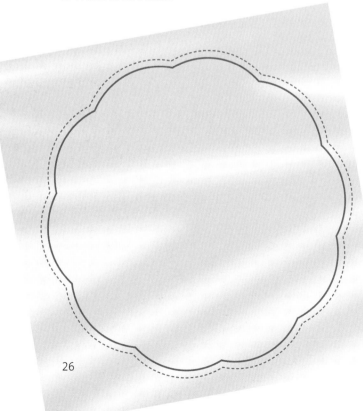

Vanity case

MATERIALS REQUIRED

- 64 x 21cm (25$^1/_4$ x 8$^1/_4$in) thin oilcloth in white
- 64 x 21cm (25$^1/_4$ x 8$^1/_4$in) thick oilcloth with a cherry blossom motif
- 1m (40in) long scoubidou strands in pearlized pastel colourways
- Fine leather needle with triangular point
- White sewing thread
- Hole punch
- Repositionable spray adhesive
- Superglue
- Double-sided tape
- Pencil
- A3 sheet of tracing paper
- Rotary cutter
- Cutting mat
- Flat metal ruler
- All-purpose scissors
- Iron
- White cotton cloth

1. PREPARATION

Enlarge the patterns by 100 per cent to twice their size. Copy the side Pattern 1 twice and the large Pattern 2 once on to tracing paper and cut them out. Take the two rectangles of oilcloth and iron them, placing a clean cloth between the iron and the oilcloth. Allow the oilcloth to cool thoroughly. Lay the oilcloth rectangles on a table, wrong sides up, and transfer the three patterns on to each of them. Cut them out. Use a rotary cutter to cut the straight lines and scissors for the curves.

2. BACKING THE PIECES

Spray a little adhesive on to the back of the three pieces of white oilcloth and position the pieces of printed oilcloth on top. Smooth out gently with a clean cloth to prevent air bubbles and creases. If the two pieces of oilcloth do not fit exactly on top of one another, the repositionable adhesive will let you peel them apart and start again.

3. PUTTING THE CASE TOGETHER

Lay Pattern 2 white side up and place one of the Pattern 1 pieces, patterned side down, on top, matching section C with section B. Sew together with a running stitch (see page 15) so the seams are on the outside. Sew section F to G and H to E in the same way. When you come to the top of the side pieces, carry on sewing across the top edge. Repeat for the other side of the case. Finish by continuing the running stitch round the two curved parts and along the top of the back and front of the case so the stitching is continuous.

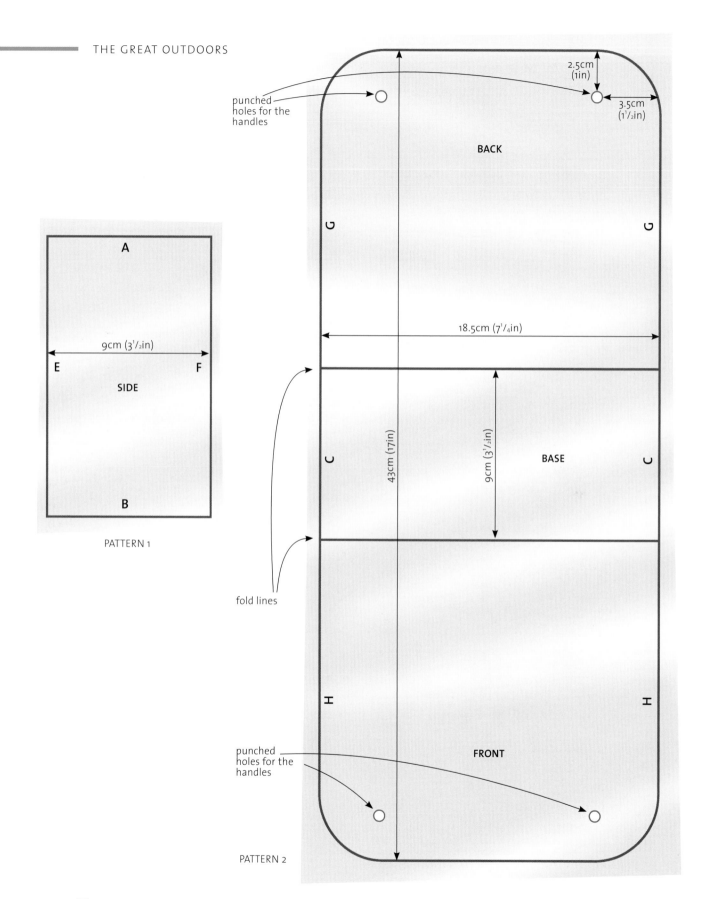

punched holes for the handles

2.5cm (1in)

3.5cm (1½in)

BACK

G

G

18.5cm (7¼in)

A

9cm (3½in)

E   F

SIDE

B

PATTERN 1

fold lines

C

43cm (17in)

9cm (3½in)

BASE

C

H

H

FRONT

punched holes for the handles

PATTERN 2

4. MAKING THE HANDLES

Use a hole punch to punch two holes in each side of the case 2.5cm (1in) from the top edge and 3.5cm (1¹/₂in) from the side. Take four scoubidou strands and thread them from the inside through the first hole, leaving approximately 12cm (4³/₄in) scoubidou inside the case. Tie the four strands together tightly inside the case. Thread the scoubidou strands back through the second hole. Tie the strands inside the case as before, then trim any excess. Make up the second handle in the same way.

5. DECORATING THE CASE

Cut six strands 13cm (5¹/₄in) long from a scoubidou strand in the colour of your choice. Tie them tightly in pairs at both ends to give you a total length of 6cm (2¹/₂in). Attach the three straps to the front of the case with superglue, keeping them centred and the same distance apart. Position the first strap 7cm (2³/₄in) from the top edge.

My outdoor jacket

MATERIALS REQUIRED

(for a pink fleece-lined rain jacket, size 4–6 years)

- 65 x 25cm (25$^{1}/_{2}$ x 10in) of coated fabric in lilac
- 13cm (5$^{1}/_{4}$in) square of coated gingham in apple green
- 9 large flower-shaped buttons 4cm (1$^{5}/_{8}$in) in diameter in fuchsia, white, purple and lilac
- Seam ripper
- All-purpose scissors and embroidery scissors

- Pale green sewing thread
- Pink sewing thread to match the jacket
- Needle
- 2 A3 sheets of tracing paper
- Pencil
- Stuffing
- 35cm (13$^{3}/_{4}$in) scoubidou strand in a pearlized light green
- Double-sided tape

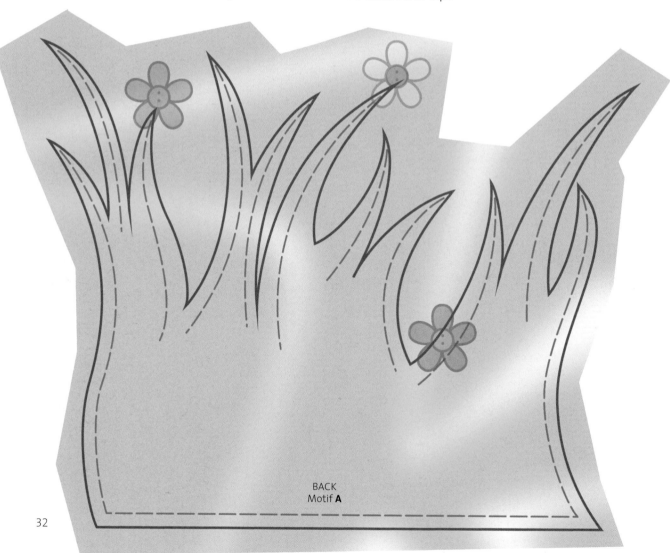

BACK
Motif **A**

1. PREPARATION

Using a seam ripper, start by undoing the seam along the bottom of the jacket so that it is separated from its lining. Enlarge the five motifs by 60 per cent using a photocopier. Copy all the motifs on to tracing paper and cut them out. Lay the lilac coated fabric wrong side up and transfer the four grass motifs on to it. Make two copies of the large flower on the wrong side of the coated gingham, turning the tracing paper over to make the second copy.

Carefully cut out all the motifs using embroidery scissors.

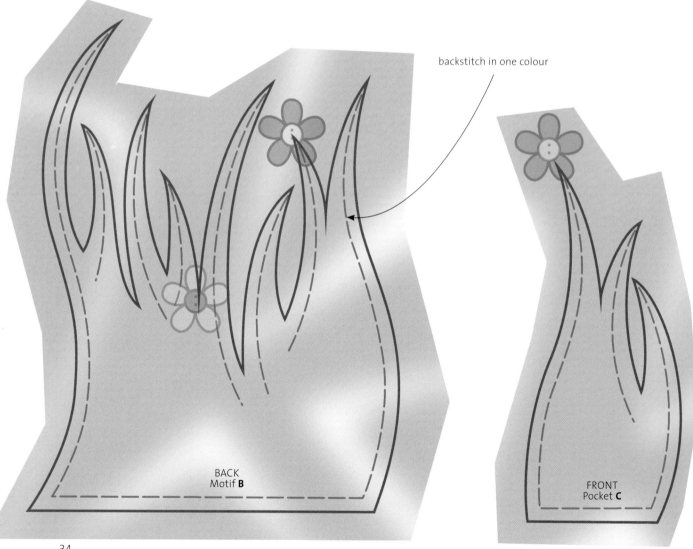

backstitch in one colour

BACK
Motif **B**

FRONT
Pocket **C**

2. MAKING THE FLOWER

Place the two flower cut-outs wrong sides together and, using pale green sewing thread, sew them together with a small running stitch (see page 15). When you get two-thirds of the way around the flower, stuff each of the petals you have sewn. Continue to sew, stuffing the remaining petals as you go, without stuffing the centre. When you have finished, sew a fuchsia button into the centre of the flower using pale green sewing thread.

3. DECORATING THE BACK OF THE JACKET

Starting 4cm (1⅝in) in from the side seam, place motif A on the back of the jacket and hold in place with a piece of double-sided tape 1cm (½in) from the bottom edge. Using green thread and a small backstitch (see page 15) sew it on following the lines on the diagram. Sew on three flower-shaped buttons with the pale green thread as positioned in the diagram. Leave a 7cm (2¾in) gap along the bottom of the jacket and sew on motif B using the same technique.

FRONT
Pocket **D**

4. ATTACHING THE FLOWER

Attach a scoubidou strand using a couching stitch (see page 15) between motifs A and B. Curve the stem and secure it with pale green thread. Attach the flower to the end of the stem with two stitches at the end of each petal, over the top of the ones you have already made. Do the same in the centre of the button.

5. DECORATING THE FRONT OF THE JACKET

Start by sewing a white flower button into the centre of the pocket on the side of your choice. Sew on motifs C and D using the same technique as for motifs A and B. Finish by sewing on the flower buttons as indicated in the diagram.

6. FINISHING TOUCHES

Once you have sewn on all the motifs and flowers, sew the bottom of the jacket back together with a slipstitch using a matching thread. Then work a very small backstitch (see page 15) to imitate a machine topstitching.

Child's picnic tablecloth

MATERIALS REQUIRED

- 100cm (40in) square of gingham oilcloth in sky blue
- 100cm (40in) square of gingham oilcloth in red with strawberry bunch motif
- 110 x 50cm (43$\frac{1}{4}$ x 20in) of coated gingham in light brown
- Red sewing thread to match the oilcloth
- Sewing thread in white and light brown
- Needle
- Pins
- Tape measure
- Long ruler
- All-purpose scissors
- Tracing paper
- Soft pencil
- Sewing machine
- Iron
- White cotton cloth
- Sticky tape
- Double-sided tape

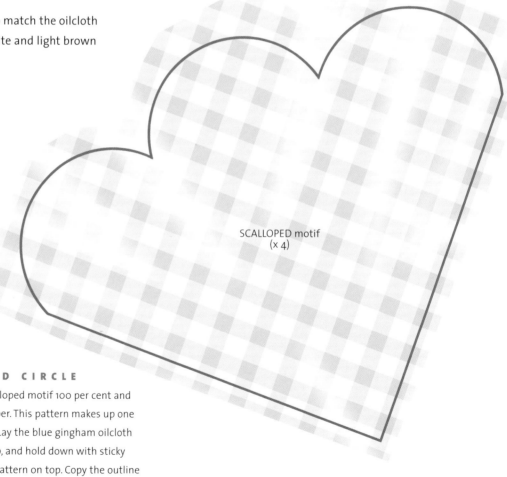

SCALLOPED motif
(x 4)

1. PREPARING THE SCALLOPED CIRCLE

Start by enlarging the scalloped motif 100 per cent and cut it out from tracing paper. This pattern makes up one quarter of the tablecloth. Lay the blue gingham oilcloth on the floor, wrong side up, and hold down with sticky tape. Place the scalloped pattern on top. Copy the outline four times in pencil, moving the template to give you a complete circle that is scalloped all the way around. Cut the tablecloth out carefully.

2. PREPARING THE HEARTS

Enlarge the heart pattern by 25 per cent, copy it on to tracing paper and cut it out. Roughly cut out 12 strawberry bunches from the red gingham oilcloth, ensuring that the pieces are larger than the heart template. Place the tracing paper heart on to the strawberry bunches, right side facing up. Copy the outline of the heart around the strawberries on the right side using a pencil. To add variety, change the way the strawberries are framed each time. Cut out the 12 hearts just inside the pencil line. If any pencil marks remain, remove them immediately with a damp sponge and a little soap, and dry the oilcloth.

3. PREPARING THE PLEATED FRILL

Mark out 12 strips 3.5cm (1¹⁄₂in) wide and 102cm (40¹⁄₄in) long on the rectangle of coated fabric with the aid of a ruler. Cut them out.

4. SEWING ON THE HEARTS

Place the oilcloth tablecloth on the floor, right side up. Position the hearts one at a time in the centre of each scalloped section. Secure with a small piece of double-sided tape at the bottom, close to the point of the heart, to stop them sliding around when you come to sew them.

Machine-sew on the heart pockets using red thread, referring to the red dotted line, which shows where to start and finish sewing. Work slowly because you are working with two layers, on the right side which sticks more than the reverse, and on curved lines: three good reasons to go easy on the sewing machine pedal!

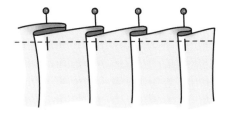

5. MAKING THE PLEATED FRILL

To make the pleats, fold a strip of the coated fabric over by 1cm ($^1/_2$in). Pin the fold at the top at the cut edge. Leave 2cm ($^7/_8$in), then fold the coated fabric over again by 1cm ($^1/_2$in). Repeat this process until the whole strip is pleated. To fix the pleats, iron the back of the strip on the cotton setting, placing a clean cloth between the iron and the coated fabric. Using light brown thread, secure all the pleats 3mm ($^1/_8$in) from the upper edge with a small backstitch (see page 15). Remove the pins as you go. Repeat for the other 11 strips.

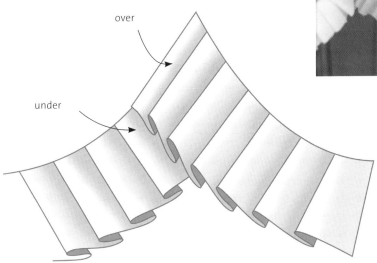

over

under

6. ATTACHING THE FRILL

Slide the first pleated strip under one of the scalloped sections and secure with a small running stitch (see page 15) using white sewing thread. When you come to sew on the second strip, start it from underneath the first, so the strips overlap slightly.

Floral apron

MATERIALS REQUIRED

- 95 x 85cm (37$\frac{1}{2}$ x 33$\frac{1}{2}$in) pink oilcloth with large coloured flowers
- 33 x 28cm (13 x 11in) gingham oilcloth in soft green
- 4.5m (5yd) bias binding in pale pink
- Sewing thread in pale pink
- All-purpose scissors
- Sewing machine
- 40cm (16in) ruler
- Tape measure
- Superglue
- Pencil
- Pins
- Iron
- White cotton cloth

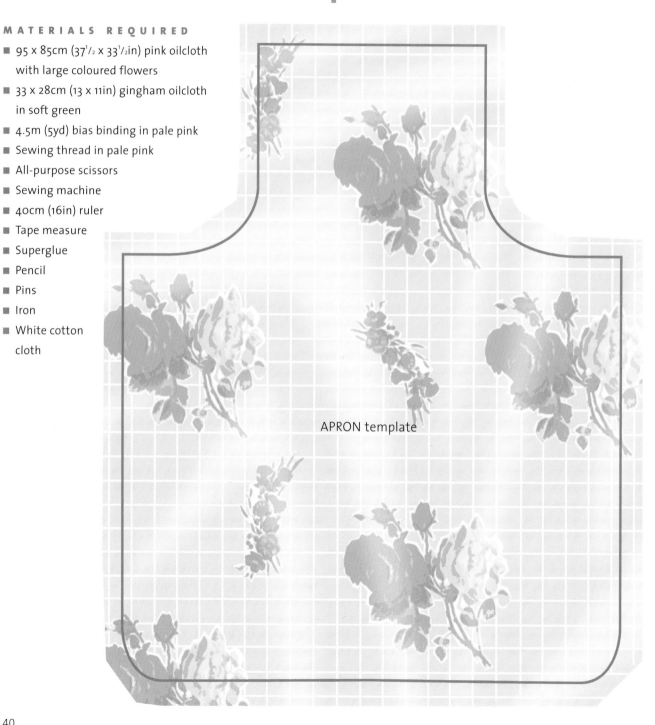

APRON template

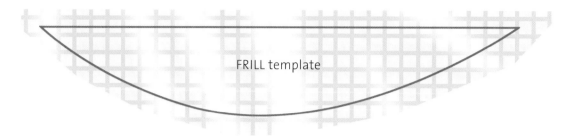

FRILL template

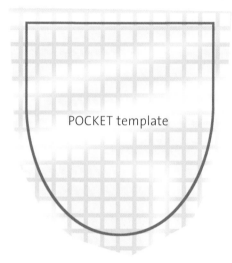

POCKET template

1. PREPARING AND CUTTING OUT THE MATERIALS

Enlarge the apron pattern by 350 per cent and the patterns for the pockets and frills by 120 per cent. Cut them out. Lay the flower-patterned oilcloth wrong side up. Place the apron pattern on top, leaving enough room to cut two 59 x 11cm (23^1/$_4$ x 4^3/$_8$in) rectangles for the straps. When you have worked out how to divide your material, transfer the apron pattern on to the oilcloth, marking the straight lines with the aid of a ruler. Cut two small bunches of flowers for the pockets from the offcuts. Lay the green gingham oilcloth wrong side up and transfer the outlines of two pockets and two frills on to it. Cut out all the pieces.

2. ADDING THE BIAS BINDING

Fold the bias binding in half lengthways and press the fold with an iron. Position it over the side edge of the apron, starting at ① on the diagram opposite and pin to secure down the side, across the bottom and up the other side. Machine-stitch using pink thread. Next, sew the bias tape round the two armholes, starting at ② and leaving 65cm

(25^1/$_2$in) excess bias binding on each side. Finish by sewing the bias binding round the two pockets ③. Refer to the diagram for all these steps.

3. MAKING THE STRAPS

Cut two 59 x 11cm (23^1/$_4$ x 4^3/$_8$in) strips from the offcuts of flower-patterned oilcloth. For each strip, fold in 1cm (^{1}/$_2$in), wrong sides together, on each long side, then fold the strip in half. This will give you two strips 4.5cm (1^3/$_4$in) wide. Pin together at 10cm (4in) intervals and machine-stitch down one of the sides 3mm (^{1}/$_8$in) from the edge using pink thread. Sew another seam the same distance from the other side to match. Make a 3cm (1^1/$_4$in) loop at one of the short ends of each strip. Sew 5mm (^{1}/$_4$in) from the edge.

green gingham flounces and sew them to each strap by hand with a running stitch (see page 15) along the seam on the straps. If you make your stitches the same length as the machine stitching they will not be seen. Use the same technique to sew on the pockets.

6. FINISHING TOUCHES

Glue two small cut-out bunches of flowers to the centre of each pocket. To put on your apron, thread the bias binding through the loops in the straps, adjust to fit and tie. This will stop the straps slipping off your shoulders.

4. MAKING THE SHOULDER FRILLS

Lay the two pieces of green gingham oilcloth right sides up. Make six pleats on each frill as follows: start at the left 4cm (1⁵/₈in) from the edge and make your first pleat by folding 5mm (¹/₄in) of oilcloth to the right. Leave 2.5cm (1in) and make a second pleat. Leave 3cm (1¹/₄in) and make a third pleat. Leave 4cm (1⁵/₈in) and make the fourth pleat. Make the fifth pleat at 3cm (1¹/₄in) and the final pleat at 2.5cm (1in). Press the pleats with your nail and secure with a few stitches.

5. PUTTING THE PIECES TOGETHER

On the reverse of the apron, lay the two short ends of the straps without loops on either side of the bib, right side to wrong side. Sew approximately 5mm (¹/₄in) from the edge. Next, add the bias binding along the top of the apron ④. This will hide the stitching on the straps. Take the two

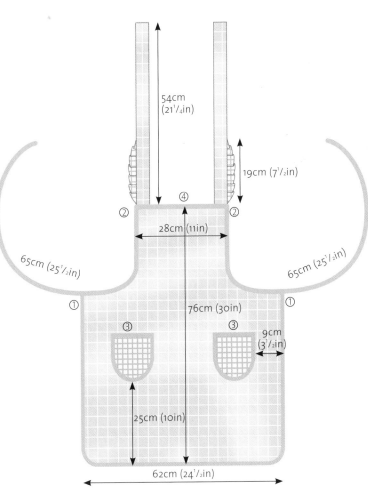

54cm (21¹/₄in)

19cm (7¹/₂in)

② ②

28cm (11in)

65cm (25¹/₂in)

65cm (25¹/₂in)

① 76cm (30in) ①

③ ③

9cm (3¹/₂in)

25cm (10in)

62cm (24¹/₂in)

Sleepover bag

MATERIALS REQUIRED

- 40 x 80cm (16 x 31$\frac{1}{2}$in) white oilcloth with blue polka dots
- Offcuts of multicoloured plain and patterned oilcloth
- 2 flower-shaped mother-of-pearl buttons in lime green
- 24cm (9$\frac{1}{2}$in) white bias binding with blue polka dots
- Miniature teddy bear
- A4 sheet of tracing paper
- Pencil
- Blue perle cotton
- Fine leather needle with triangular point
- White sewing thread
- Sewing machine
- All-purpose scissors
- Embroidery scissors
- Superglue
- Pins
- Tape measure
- Paper clips
- 40cm (16in) ruler and set square
- 1 white self-adhesive Velcro circle 1cm ($\frac{1}{2}$in) in diameter

1. PREPARING THE BAG PARTS

Using a set square and ruler, start by drawing a rectangle 72 x 32cm (28$\frac{1}{2}$ x 12$\frac{1}{2}$in) on the back of the oilcloth. This will be the main section of the bag. Draw two strips 49 x 7cm (19$\frac{1}{4}$ x 2$\frac{3}{4}$in) for the handles, and one strip 23 x 5cm (9 x 2in) and another 17 x 5cm (6$\frac{3}{4}$ x 2in) for the toothbrush pouch on the remaining oilcloth. Cut out all these pieces.

2. PREPARING THE DECORATIONS

Copy the three flowers, the two leaves and the three circles for the centres of the flowers on to tracing paper. Place the patterned offcuts wrong side up and draw round the outlines of the flowers and the leaves, making two copies of the smallest flower. Do the same with the offcuts of plain oilcloth for the centres of the four flowers. Cut out all the motifs with embroidery scissors, then superglue a centre on to each flower. Leave to dry.

3. SEWING THE BAG TOGETHER

Take the large oilcloth rectangle and fold it in half, right sides together. Draw a line 1cm ($^1/_2$in) from the edge of the long sides using a ruler and pencil. Pin close to each edge at approximately 8cm ($3^1/_4$in) intervals. Machine-sew.

To make the base of the bag, flatten out the side seams and place them over the fold across the bottom of the bag to make a triangle 4cm ($1^5/_8$in) high and with an 8cm ($3^1/_4$in) base. Using a pencil, mark the 8cm ($3^1/_4$in) lines and machine-sew. Use the diagram as a guide if necessary.

4. SEWING THE HANDLES

Lay the two 49 x 7cm ($19^1/_4$ x $2^3/_4$in) strips wrong side up. Fold over 1cm ($^1/_2$in) to the wrong sides along both the long sides. Press these folds with your nail, then fold each strip in half to make strips 2.5cm (1in) wide. Hold the folded strips in place with paper clips and machine-stitch 5mm ($^1/_4$in) from the edge, removing the paper clips as you go. Stitch a second row on the other side, again 5mm ($^1/_4$in) from the edge, to match.

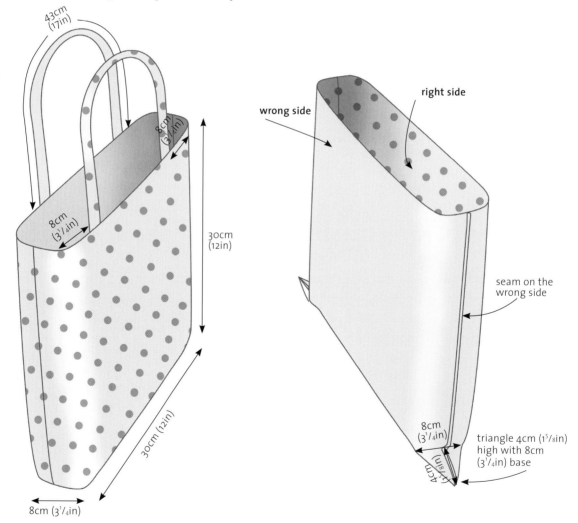

43cm (17in)

8cm ($3^1/_4$in)

8cm ($3^1/_4$in)

30cm (12in)

30cm (12in)

8cm ($3^1/_4$in)

wrong side

right side

seam on the wrong side

8cm ($3^1/_4$in)

4cm ($1^5/_8$in)

triangle 4cm ($1^5/_8$in) high with 8cm ($3^1/_4$in) base

5. ATTACHING THE HANDLES TO THE BAG

Fold 2cm ($^7/_8$in) of the upper edge of the bag to the inside and hold in place with paper clips. Position the handles on the inside of the bag, pinning them 8cm ($3^1/_4$in) from the side seams with a 9cm ($3^1/_2$in) gap between. Sew all the way around the bag by machine, approximately 1.5cm ($^3/_4$in) from the edge, to secure the handles as well as the inside flap. This technique is only suitable for small bags that are not designed to carry heavy items.

Should you require a stronger bag, reinforce the stitching by going over the handles again by hand using invisible nylon thread and sewing only through the flap, so as not to make holes in the right side of the fabric. Turn the bag right side out and sew two buttons to the base of the front handles, as high as possible.

6. TOOTHBRUSH POUCH

Use a triangular-pointed leather needle to sew the teddy bear on to the bottom of the small oilcloth rectangle, in the centre. Attach this rectangle to the larger one using perle cotton and blanket stitch (see page 15) to sew all the way around.

Pass the polka dot tape around one of the bag handles and attach the two ends to the back of the pouch, taking care to only go through the back and not through the front.

Fold down the flap at the top, pressing it with your nail, and glue one of the small flowers to the centre of the flap. Finish by sticking on the two halves of the Velcro circle, one on the front of the pouch at the top and the other under the flap to match, and close the pouch.

7. FINISHING TOUCHES

Put some newspapers in the bag to give you a firm backing while you position the other three flowers and the leaf motifs and glue them on.

Leave to dry flat for two hours.

VINTAGE CHIC

Gingham storage jar

MATERIALS REQUIRED

(for a storage jar 17cm (6³/₄in) tall and 11cm (4³/₈in) in diameter)

- 24 x 42cm (9¹/₂ x 16¹/₂in) blue coated gingham
- 11 x 42cm (4³/₈ x 16¹/₂in) raspberry oilcloth
- Rug hook (or latch hook)
- Needle
- Pins
- Strong fabric glue
- Double-sided tape
- Pencil
- Tracing paper
- Rotary cutter
- Cutting mat
- Flat metal ruler
- Iron
- White cotton cloth

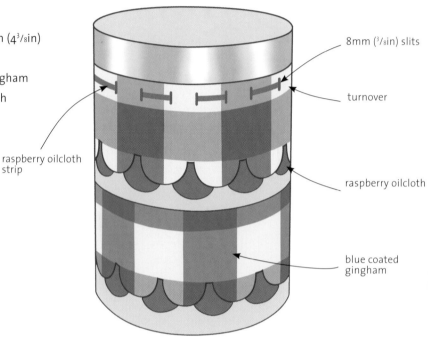

8mm (³/₈in) slits

turnover

raspberry oilcloth strip

raspberry oilcloth

blue coated gingham

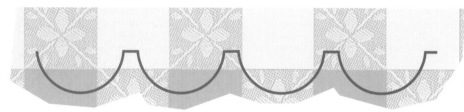

1. MAKING THE SCALLOPED STRIPS

Using a rotary cutter and cutting mat, cut two 39 x 10cm (15¹/₂ x 4in) strips from the blue coated gingham. Ensure there are four full squares across the width of the strips. Copy the scalloped motif on to tracing paper. Transfer the outline on to the back of the two strips of blue coated gingham, moving the tracing paper as you go. Cut out. Lay the raspberry oilcloth wrong side up and draw two scalloped strips 39 x 4cm (15¹/₂ x 1⁵/₈in). Cut a narrow strip 39 x 3mm (15¹/₂ x ¹/₈in) from the offcuts.

2. ASSEMBLING THE STRIPS

Lay the two gingham strips wrong side up and place a raspberry oilcloth strip, also wrong side up, on top of each one along the bottom. The raspberry oilcloth should overhang the gingham by about 5mm (¹/₄in). Alternate the scallops so the raspberry oilcloth scallops appear in the gaps between the gingham scallops. Hold the two strips together with small pieces of double-sided tape. Once both two-layer strips are assembled, turn over 1.5cm (³/₄in) at the top of the oilcloth. Press with an iron to mark the fold, placing a clean cloth between the coated fabric and the iron. Secure with a little fabric glue.

3. ATTACHING THE THIN STRIP

Take the strip for the top of the storage jar and make 8mm (³/₈in) vertical slits every 2cm (⁷/₈in) in the centre of the turnover. Thread the raspberry oilcloth strip through the slits using a rug or latch hook.

4. FINISHING OFF

Place the top strip around the storage jar. Mark where the seam will go with two pins. Remove the strip and backstitch (see page 15) to join the ends. Trim the excess oilcloth. Replace the strip, sliding it over the base of the storage jar. Repeat this process with the second strip.

Recipe notebook

MATERIALS REQUIRED

(for a notebook 18.5cm (7$^{1}/_{4}$in) square)

- 25cm (10in) square red coated gingham
- 21 x 54cm (8$^{1}/_{4}$ x 21$^{1}/_{4}$in) coated gingham in ivory shades
- 4 self-cover buttons 19mm ($^{3}/_{4}$in) diameter
- 1 self-cover button 23mm (1in) diameter
- Needle
- Ivory sewing thread
- All-purpose solvent-free adhesive
- Synthetic paintbrush
- 2 small clothes pegs
- Pencil
- Tracing paper
- Cutting mat
- Flat metal ruler
- Rotary cutter
- All-purpose scissors
- Iron
- White cotton cloth

1. MAKING THE COVER

Cut a rectangle 19.2 x 49cm (7$^{5}/_{8}$ x 19$^{1}/_{4}$in) from the ivory coated fabric. For neat lines, use a rotary cutter on a cutting mat.

At each end of the rectangle use an iron to press a 4.3cm (1$^{3}/_{4}$in) fold to the wrong side. Remember to place a clean cloth between the iron and the coated fabric.

Using ivory thread, sew the top and bottom of the fold on the right side with a running stitch (see page 15) 1mm ($^{1}/_{16}$in) from the edge. Try the cover for size and take it off.

2. MAKING THE SCALLOPED MOTIF

Copy the scalloped motif on to tracing paper and cut it out. Lay the red coated gingham rectangle wrong side up and draw a strip 14 x 19cm (5$^{1}/_{2}$ x 7$^{1}/_{2}$in). Use the template to draw scallops along both long edges, moving the tracing paper as you go. Cut the top and bottom of the strip with a rotary cutter and then cut the scalloping out with scissors.

3. MAKING AND ADDING THE BUTTONS

Following the manufacturer's instructions, cover the four small buttons in offcuts of red gingham, alternating between dark and light squares of the oilcloth. Cover the 23mm (1in) diameter button in the same way. Sew the four small buttons on to one scalloped edge, alternating light and dark buttons. Sew the large button on to the front of the ivory coated fabric cover, centred vertically, 2cm ($^{7}/_{8}$in) from the outside edge.

4. ASSEMBLY

Fold the ivory case and the red gingham scalloped strip in half and gently mark the folds with your nail. Apply glue to the back of the scalloped strip with a paintbrush and stick it on to the cover, ensuring that the central fold marks match. Hold at the top and bottom with two small clothes pegs and leave to dry for two hours before putting the notebook in its cover.

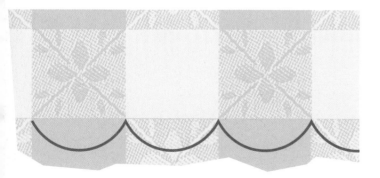

Jam jar hats

MATERIALS REQUIRED

(to make 2 jar tops)

- 2 jam jars 9.5cm (3³/₄in) in diameter
- 23cm (9in) square raspberry oilcloth
- 23cm (9in) square white oilcloth
- 20cm (8in) square red gingham oilcloth
- 20 x 10cm (8 x 4in) white lace-effect oilcloth
- 1.2m (48in) cord in blackcurrant
- 1.2m (48in) cord in white
- Large heart punch
- Small heart punch
- Hole punch
- Fine synthetic paintbrush
- All-purpose glue
- Scrap of cardboard packaging
- 2 sheets tracing paper
- Pencil
- Pair of compasses
- Old cloth
- All-purpose scissors

1. CUTTING OUT THE JAR TOPS

Enlarge the two templates by 50 per cent. Copy them on to tracing paper and cut out carefully. Lay the white and raspberry oilcloths wrong side up. Transfer each template on to the appropriate piece of oilcloth and cut out.

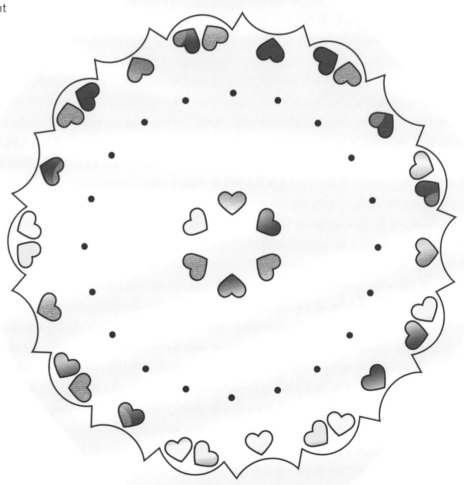

2. MAKING THE DECORATIONS

With the large heart punch, punch 14 hearts in the white lace-effect oilcloth. With the small heart punch, punch 33 hearts in the red gingham oilcloth, choosing light and dark areas so as to get as many different small hearts as possible. Use a pair of compasses to draw a circle about 3cm (1^1/$_4$in) from the outside edge on each piece and mark the position for about 20 holes all the way round the circle. Using the hole punch, punch the holes, spacing them evenly.

3. ADDING THE DECORATIONS

Position the two lid covers right sides up. Place a little glue on the scrap of cardboard and, with a paintbrush, apply glue to each of the decorative elements in turn. Be sparing and spread the glue out well over the surface of the hearts. Stick the glued hearts on to the lid covers, making sure that the glue does not seep out from the sides. If this occurs, wipe immediately with a damp cloth. Use the templates as a guide to the correct positioning of the decorations. Leave to dry for at least four hours.

4. FINISHING TOUCHES

Thread the cord through the holes. Place the lid covers on
the jars and pull gently on the cords to gather them. Tie in
a bow to hold these pretty covers in place.

Wicker shopping basket

MATERIALS REQUIRED

(for an oval basket)

- 110 x 80cm (43¹/₄ x 31¹/₂in) red coated gingham
- 2.5m (100in) red bias binding
- White sewing thread
- Red sewing thread to match the bias binding
- Pencil
- All-purpose scissors
- Tape measure
- Ruler
- Iron
- Pins and a safety pin
- Sewing machine

1. PREPARATION

Start by carefully ironing the piece of coated fabric on the reverse. Using Template A as a guide, copy the pattern for the sides twice, and use Template B to copy the pattern for the bottom of the basket lining once. Mark all the straight lines with a ruler.

2. CUTTING OUT THE PIECES

Cut out the three pieces. Mark the section outlined in red on the two side pieces. This is where the basket handle will fit. Place one of the side pieces wrong side up and mark a line 1.5cm (³/₄in) from the top edge. Place this piece on top of the other, right sides together, and draw a line on the right and left 5mm (¹/₄in) from the edge. This will serve as a guide for the stitching.

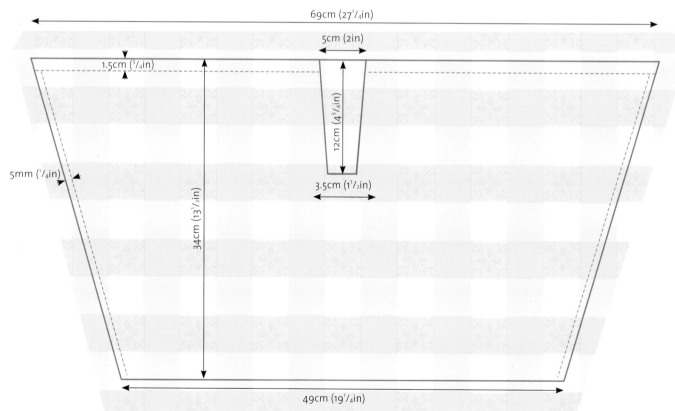

69cm (27¹/₄in)

5cm (2in)

1.5cm (³/₄in)

12cm (4³/₄in)

3.5cm (1¹/₂in)

5mm (¹/₄in)

34cm (13¹/₂in)

49cm (19¹/₄in)

TEMPLATE **A**

DIAGRAM **C**

TEMPLATE **B**

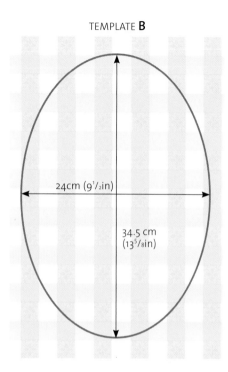

24cm (9$\frac{1}{2}$in)

34.5 cm (13$\frac{5}{8}$in)

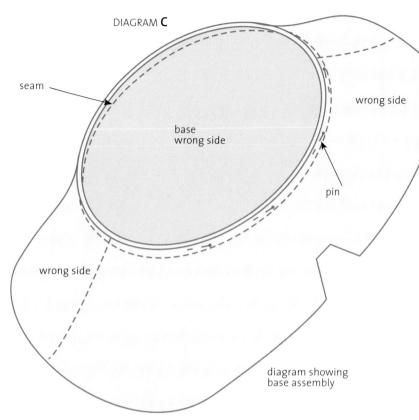

seam

wrong side

base
wrong side

pin

wrong side

diagram showing
base assembly

3. SEWING THE SIDES

Pin the two side pieces right sides together and, starting from the base, machine-sew the 5mm ($\frac{1}{4}$in) seams using white thread. Stop when you reach the horizontal line drawn 1.5cm ($\frac{3}{4}$in) from the top edge. Fold the top edge down to the wrong side and pin. Machine-sew using white sewing thread to make a 1cm ($\frac{1}{2}$in) channel.
These two sides form a ring that is now attached to the lining base.

4. ATTACHING THE BASE

Using Diagram C as a guide, pin the base to the sides, right sides together, at 2cm ($\frac{7}{8}$in) intervals. Machine-sew 5mm ($\frac{1}{4}$in) from the edge. Open out all the seams and press with an iron. Place the lining in the basket, smoothing out any folds.

5. FINISHING TOUCHES

Cut the bias binding into two pieces of equal length. Fold in half and machine-sew using red sewing thread. Attach a safety pin to the end of one of the lengths of bias binding. Using Diagram D as a guide, thread it through the lining hem. Repeat this for the second length of bias binding. Tie them together in a bow each side, below the handle.

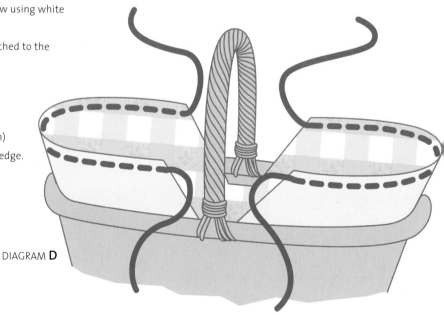

DIAGRAM **D**

Elegant flowerpot holder

MATERIALS REQUIRED

(for a zinc flowerpot 14cm (5$\frac{1}{2}$in) wide at the top, 10cm (4in) wide at the base and 14cm (5$\frac{1}{2}$in) high)

- 32 x 25cm (12$\frac{1}{2}$ x 10in) green coated gingham
- 65 x 20cm (25$\frac{1}{2}$ x 8in) white coated fabric with blue and pale green stripes
- Small piece of coated fabric in plain green or with an ivy pattern
- 2 large green beads
- 1 large white bead
- 65 x 20cm (25$\frac{1}{2}$ x 8in) iron-on fabric
- Tracing paper
- A4 paper
- Pencil
- Ruler
- All-purpose scissors
- Embroidery scissors
- Superglue
- White and pale green sewing thread
- Needle
- Iron
- Soft sponge
- Washing-up liquid
- White cotton cloth
- Sewing machine (optional)

BEFORE YOU START

Clean your flowerpot thoroughly with a soft sponge and some washing-up liquid.

Zinc will leave a blackish deposit on your fingers that could stain your coated fabric when you come to try it for size. Although coated fabric is easy to clean, it would be a shame if your creation was covered in fingerprints before you had chance to use it. When the cloth stays white after wiping you will know that the pot is completely clean.

1. PREPARING THE FLOWERPOT SIDES

Place your flowerpot on its side on a sheet of white paper and draw around it using a ruler.

Again using your ruler, add 5mm ($\frac{1}{4}$in) to the sides. Cut out the paper template and place it on the striped coated fabric, laid wrong side up. Copy the outline four times. Cut out using the all-purpose scissors. Repeat this process on the iron-on fabric and cut out. Place the shiny side of the iron-on fabric on the wrong side of the coated fabric and iron to attach.

Use a ruler to draw a line 5mm ($\frac{1}{4}$in) from the side edges on each piece of iron-on fabric, to keep your stitching neat.

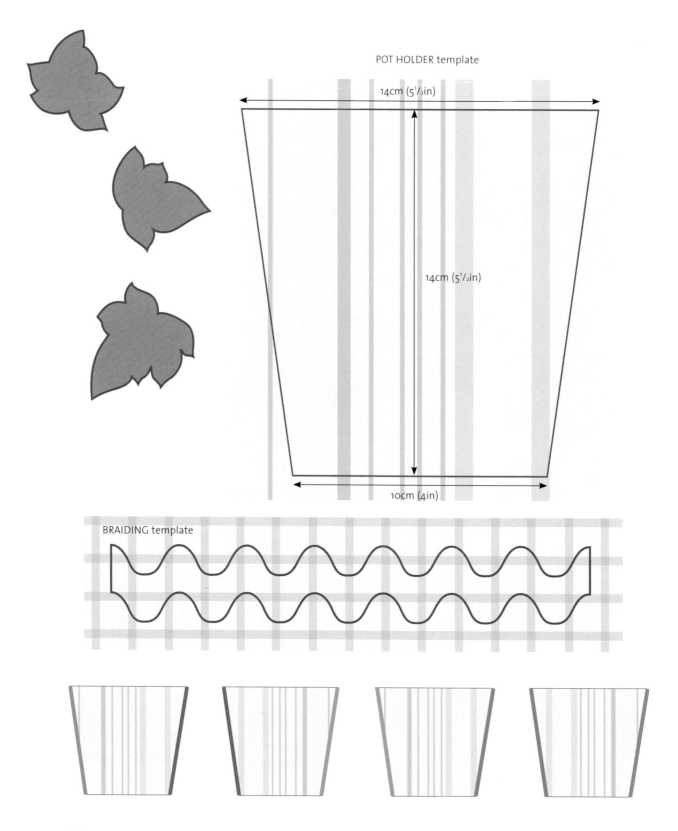

POT HOLDER template

14cm (5½in)

14cm (5½in)

10cm (4in)

BRAIDING template

Glue the leaves and flowers on to the right side of one of the sides of the sleeve, using the photo as a guide. Glue the four strips of braiding along the upper edges so they overlap at their halfway point. Leave to dry for two hours and slide the sleeve on to the flowerpot from the base.

2. PREPARING THE BRAIDING AND THE FLOWERS

Copy the braiding template on to tracing paper and cut out the pattern. Place it on the wrong side of the green coated gingham and copy the outline four times, moving the tracing paper to give you four pieces 14cm (5^1/$_2$in) in length. To make the flowers, copy the equivalent of 5^1/$_2$ braiding 'teeth' three times. Cut out the pieces of braiding carefully with embroidery scissors.

3. PUTTING THE SLEEVE TOGETHER

With the right sides of the striped fabric facing, sew the four sides of the flowerpot holder together with white sewing thread, either by machine or by hand, using a small, very narrow backstitch (see page 15). Use the coloured lines on the diagram opposite to help you.

4. MAKING THE BRAID FLOWERS

Tie a knot at the end of a needle threaded with green sewing thread and insert the needle under a 'tooth'. Go under the next tooth to make a circle. Fold the two half-teeth to the reverse and join them with a few stitches. Attach a green or white bead to the centre of each finished flower. Make up the three flowers in this way.

5. MAKING THE LEAVES

Cut out five ivy leaves of varying sizes from an ivy-patterned oilcloth or use the templates to make your own from plain green oilcloth. To do this, copy the leaves on to tracing paper, transfer their outlines on to the back of the oilcloth and cut them out using embroidery scissors.

Camellia bag

MATERIALS REQUIRED

- 80 x 55cm (31¹/₂in x 21³/₄in) fairly thin white oilcloth with flower pattern
- 70 x 35cm (27⁵/₈ x 13³/₄in) light beige coated fabric
- 50 x 25cm (20 x 10in) white coated fabric
- 96cm (37³/₄in) white cord 1cm (¹/₂in) in diameter
- A4 sheet of paper
- Pair of compasses
- Pencil
- Long ruler
- Tape measure
- Pins
- All-purpose scissors
- Iron
- White cotton cloth
- White and light beige sewing thread
- Needle
- Fine leather needle with triangular point
- Sewing machine

1. PREPARING THE BAG PIECES

Lay the oilcloth wrong side up. Using the pattern as a guide, mark the outline of the main section of the bag with a pencil and ruler. Cut out. Draw two strips 52 x 7cm (20¹/₂ x 2³/₄in) in the offcut, which will make the handles. Cut them out.

2. PREPARING THE FLOWERS

With a pair of compasses, mark out nine circles 9.5cm (3³/₄in) in diameter on the wrong side of the beige coated fabric. Lay the piece of white coated fabric wrong side up and mark out 12 circles 6.5cm (2⁵/₈in) in diameter. Cut out the white and beige circles carefully just inside the lines so that no pencil marks remain.

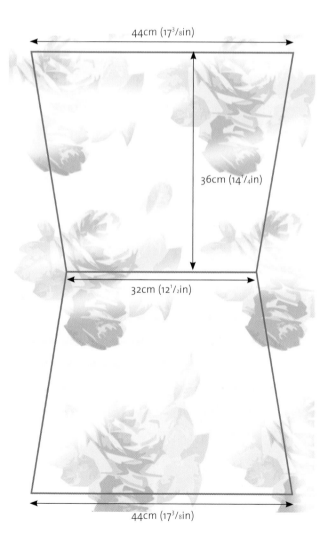

44cm (17³/₈in)

36cm (14¹/₄in)

32cm (12¹/₂in)

44cm (17³/₈in)

3. MAKING THE HANDLES

Lay one strip of oilcloth wrong side up and fold 1cm ($^1/_2$in) over, wrong sides together, along one long edge. Place the cotton cloth on the fold and press with a cool iron. Take care not to melt the oilcloth with too hot an iron.
Place the cord in the centre of the strip. There should be 2cm ($^7/_8$in) excess oilcloth at each end. Fold the two long edges over the cord so the side with the flap covers the other side. Pin at 2cm ($^7/_8$in) intervals and secure with a very small slipstitch. Repeat for the second handle.

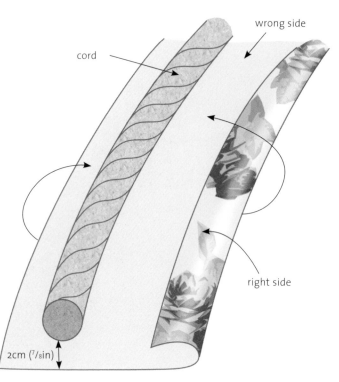

wrong side

cord

right side

2cm ($^7/_8$in)

4. BAG ASSEMBLY

Take the piece of oilcloth you have cut out for the bag and fold it in half, right sides together. Draw a line 1cm ($^1/_2$in) from the edge along the sides with a ruler and pencil. Pin close to each edge roughly every 8cm ($3^1/_4$in) and then machine-sew along the drawn lines.

5. SHAPING THE BAG

To shape the bottom of the bag, flatten out the side seams and place them over the fold in the bottom of the bag to make a triangle 4cm ($1^5/_8$in) high with an 8cm ($3^1/_4$in) base. Mark the 8cm ($3^1/_4$in) lines in pencil and machine-sew. Refer to the diagram for the Sleepover bag on page 44 if necessary.

6. ATTACHING THE HANDLES TO THE BAG

Fold the top edge of your bag 3cm ($1^1/_4$in) to the wrong side and hold in place with paper clips. Place the handles, one on each side, on the wrong side of the bag and pin them 10cm (4in) from the side seams. Leave an 18cm ($7^1/_8$in) gap between the handles. Machine-sew all the way around approximately 1cm ($^1/_2$in) from the edge. This will fix both the handles and the inside flap. Turn the bag out.

48cm (19in)

18cm ($7^1/_8$in)

10cm (4in)

30cm (12in)

22cm ($8^3/_4$in)

8cm ($3^1/_4$in)

7. MAKING THE FLOWERS

Make the flowers as follows: fold a circle of coated fabric into four. Secure it folded with a couple of strong stitches at the base of the triangle you have made using a thread to match the colour of the coated fabric. Repeat this process on two other circles. Sew the three triangles together at the base with firm stitches to make the flower. Make up three large beige flowers and four small white flowers in this way.

8. SEWING FLOWERS ON THE BAG

Start by sewing on one small white flower 7cm (2³/₄in) from the side seam. Attach it 2cm (⁷/₈in) from the top edge of the bag so that the petals overlap the edge. Sew on the remaining flowers, alternating between beige and white flowers as you go.

Exotic place mats

MATERIALS REQUIRED (to make two place mats)

- 90 x 50cm (35$\frac{1}{2}$ x 20in) white oilcloth
- 100 x 16cm (40 x 6$\frac{1}{2}$in) coated damask in almond green
- 40 x 11cm (16 x 4$\frac{3}{8}$in) coated damask in white
- Pencil
- 2 sheets A3 tracing paper
- 1 sheet A4 tracing paper
- Double-sided tape
- Sticky tape
- All-purpose scissors
- Embroidery scissors
- Small pair wire cutters
- Fabric glue
- Superglue
- Copper wire 28mm in diameter
- Fine synthetic paintbrush
- Iron
- White cotton cloth
- White self-adhesive Velcro circles 1cm ($\frac{1}{2}$in) in diameter (optional)

Flower 3

Flower 1

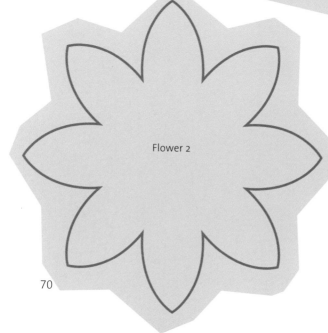

Flower 2

1. PREPARING THE TEMPLATES

Start by photocopying the leaf template (see page 73) by 100 per cent to twice its size. Take the two sheets of A3 tracing paper and join them together with sticky tape. Copy the leaf pattern on to the tracing paper. The flower templates are shown actual size. Transfer the outlines of the flowers directly on to the sheet of A4 tracing paper.

2. CUTTING OUT THE LEAVES

Lay the piece of white oilcloth wrong side up. Take the leaf template and copy the outline once. Turn the tracing paper over to draw the second leaf. Cut the two leaves out inside the lines so no pencil marks remain using a pair of all-purpose scissors.

3. CUTTING OUT THE FLOWERS

Lay the green damask fabric wrong side up and make four copies of flower 1 and four copies of flower 2. With the white damask fabric wrong side up make four copies of flower 3.

Carefully cut out all the flowers inside the lines using embroidery scissors.

4. MAKING THE LOTUS FLOWERS

Start by ironing all the shapes you have cut out on the reverse, placing a clean white cloth between the coated fabric and the iron. Leave to cool for 10 minutes.

Take one flower 1 (it should be green) and place it wrong side up. Using the diagram as a guide, stick eight strips of double-sided tape about 4.5cm (1³/₄in) long in a star shape. Use wire cutters to cut eight short pieces of copper wire

to the same length. Stick a length of copper wire to each piece of tape.

Using a synthetic paintbrush and fabric glue, lightly coat the back of the flower, except for the areas of tape and copper wire. Take a second flower 1 and place it wrong sides together on the glue-coated flower. Smooth gently with a clean white cloth to remove creases. Leave to dry for at least three hours, then curve the petals gently towards the centre.

Repeat these steps for green flower 2 and for the small white flower 3. When all the flowers are dry, assemble them by putting flower 3 into flower 2 and flower 2 into flower 1 using a dab of superglue to hold each layer. Sit your lotus flower on the place mat leaf or secure it with a Velcro circle. This will allow you to remove the lotus when you clean or store your place mats.

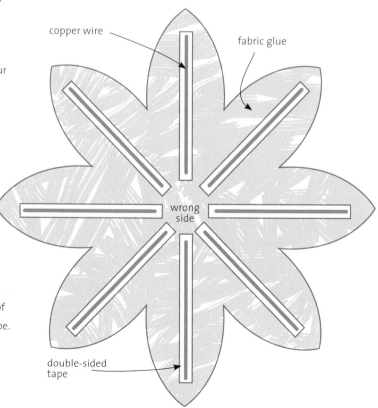

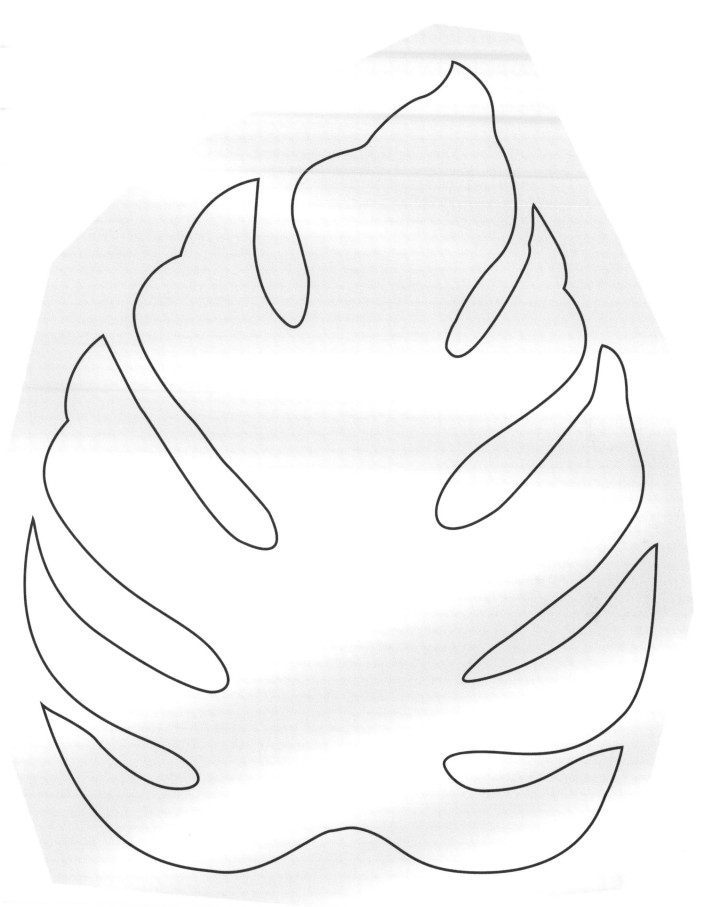

Toile de jouy dishes

MATERIALS REQUIRED

(for four transparent dessert plates)

- 40cm (16in) square blue toile de jouy oilcloth
- 2 sheets A4 tracing paper
- Pencil
- Pair of compasses
- Repositionable sticky tape
- Ruler
- All-purpose scissors
- 1 bottle surface preparation medium
- 1 cloth
- Glass paint in various shades of blue and violet
- Fine synthetic paintbrush
- Synthetic paintbrush with wide, flat tip
- Varnish for glass and china

1. PREPARATION

Place the plate upside down on your table. Place a sheet of tracing paper on top. Using a pencil, trace the outline of the plate base. Measure the diameter of this circle and draw an identical circle on the second sheet of tracing paper with compasses. Cut it out.

Lay the oilcloth right side up and select four scenes, different if possible. Draw a square slightly larger than the size of the circle around each one with a pencil. Cut the four squares out.

2. CUTTING OUT THE MOTIFS

Attach one of the oilcloth squares to a well-lit window with sticky tape, wrong side facing you. Place the tracing paper circle on the back of the oilcloth; the light behind the fabric will enable you to position your motif accurately. When you have worked out how the design will appear within the circle, copy the outline of the tracing paper circle on to the oilcloth. Remove the tape and cut out the oilcloth. Do the same for the other three scenes.

3. ASSEMBLY AND FINISHING TOUCHES

Lay the four oilcloth circles right sides up and wipe them down with a cloth soaked in preparation medium. Use a fine paintbrush and glass paint to colour some areas of the design. Leave to dry for two hours and apply a layer of varnish with the flat brush. Glue the oilcloth circle on to the back of the plate. Leave to dry for another hour. Cut out a second circle, identical to the first, from an oilcloth offcut and coat the back generously with varnish. Glue this circle to the one already attached to the plate, wrong sides together, and leave to dry. These plates are essentially decorative. They can, however, be cleaned inside with a damp sponge.

Daffodil vase

MATERIALS REQUIRED

- Transparent glass vase
- 40 x 110cm (16 x 43¹/₄in) thin white lace-effect oilcloth
- A3 sheet of tracing paper
- 3 sheets white A3 paper
- Adhesive putty
- Varnish for glass and china
- Synthetic paintbrush
- Paper scissors
- Embroidery scissors
- Pencil
- Soft pencil
- Soft sponge
- Washing-up liquid
- White tea towel
- Lint-free white cloth
- Large bath towel

1. PREPARING THE PAPER MOCK-UP

This design was for a vase 36cm (14¹/₄in) tall and 21cm (8¹/₄in) in diameter at the top. Use a photocopier to enlarge the daffodil motif by 80 per cent. If your vase is smaller, reduce the percentage. Copy the motif twice on to tracing paper with a pencil. Set one copy aside and copy the motif on to the sheets of white paper as many times as you can. Cut out the flowers. It is essential to make a paper mock-up first to achieve the correct spacing between each flower: attach the flowers to the top and bottom of the vase with adhesive putty and adjust until the flowers are evenly spaced out.

2. CUTTING OUT THE FLOWERS

Lay the oilcloth wrong side up. With your paper scissors, cut out the tracing paper flower you set aside as neatly as possible.

Place it on the back of the oilcloth and draw around the outline using a soft pencil. Cut it out with embroidery scissors. Place it straight on to a flat surface and remove the soft pencil marks with a damp sponge and a little washing-up liquid. Rinse the flower well under running water. Dry by patting the flower on each side with a tea towel. Repeat this process for the number of flowers you need.

3. GLUING THE FLOWERS ON THE VASE

Carefully wash your vase in warm soapy water and dry it. Fold a bath towel into four on the table and sit the vase on top in the centre. Lift the end of one paper stem and make a small mark with the pencil. Remove the paper flower.

Using a paintbrush, apply varnish to about 6cm (2¹/₂in) of the base of the stem of the oilcloth flower. Stick it immediately on to the vase, using the mark as a guide. Glue on the rest of the flower, working in 10cm (4in) sections at most. Stick on all the flowers in this way. If varnish seeps out from the edges, remove it with a clean white cloth. Leave to dry for 24 hours.

English country tablecloth

MATERIALS REQUIRED

(for a table 57 x 77cm (22$\frac{1}{2}$ x 30$\frac{1}{4}$in))

- 140 x 115cm (55 x 45$\frac{1}{4}$in) red and pink striped oilcloth
- 140 x 115cm (55 x 45$\frac{1}{4}$in) oilcloth in the same shades with a rose pattern
- All-purpose scissors
- Embroidery scissors
- Long ruler
- Tape measure
- Set square
- Repositionable spray adhesive for fabrics
- Superglue
- Fine leather needle with triangular point
- Nylon thread 2.5mm thick

BEFORE YOU START

If you intend making this tablecloth for a table with different dimensions, measure the length and width of the table top and add 50cm (20in) to each measurement to give you a 25cm (10in) drape on each side.

If the flowers are fairly densely distributed on the floral oilcloth you should purchase the same quantity as for the striped oilcloth. If not, purchase 20–30 per cent more fabric to make the flowers for around the tablecloth and the bouquet in the centre.

1. PREPARING THE BASE

Lay the striped oilcloth rectangle on the floor, wrong side up. Using a set square and ruler, draw a rectangle the size of your table top plus an extra 50cm (20in) across the length and width. It is essential to use a set square when working with a striped pattern to avoid making a tablecloth with slanting lines. Cut the rectangle out with all-purpose scissors.

2. PREPARING THE FLOWERS

Start by roughly cutting out the motifs on the flower-patterned oilcloth using all-purpose scissors. Now get yourself comfortable because the next stage is a lengthy process. Using embroidery scissors, cut around the outlines of the flowers neatly. If there are very detailed parts of the pattern feel free to create your own shapes, or smooth out any elaborate parts. Very tiny pieces are too fragile for a tablecloth and will either come unstuck or be impossible to sew on.

3. MAKING THE BORDER AND THE BOUQUET

Lay the rectangle of striped oilcloth on the floor, right side up. Spray a little repositionable fabric adhesive on the backs of the flowers you have cut out and start to create the border around the bottom of the tablecloth. To achieve an attractive shaped edge, leave a small leaf or part of a flower hanging up to 2.5cm (1in) over the edge of the tablecloth. Avoid overlapping the flowers by more than 1cm (½in) as this makes them difficult to glue down and even more difficult to sew on. When you have finished the edge, put together the bouquet in the middle of the tablecloth, ensuring that it is well centred.

4. METHOD ONE: GLUING THE FLOWERS

When you are happy with the positioning of your flowers, you have two methods of attaching them. If your tablecloth will spend most of its time on the table you can opt for the quick method, which involves gluing on all the flowers with superglue. To do this, it is important not to undo your composition. Starting in one corner, lift the first flower, glue it down and continue in this way. This method is very fast, but you should be aware that, when used on a surface like this, the glue will make the tablecloth very stiff and it may become brittle if you later want to roll it around a tube to store it.

After the first gluing leave the tablecloth to dry for 24 hours and ensure that all the flowers are well stuck down. You will almost certainly have to re-glue some areas. Because it is such a large surface area it is hard to fix all the surfaces completely. Repeat this process if necessary, particularly in areas where the motifs join, which are the most fragile.

5. METHOD TWO: SEWING THE FLOWERS

If you need to move and store the tablecloth, it is preferable to sew the flowers on. This takes much longer but preserves the suppleness of the tablecloth and means that it can be rolled up without getting damaged. If you opt for this method, use a small backstitch (see page 15) to sew around the outline of the flowers using nylon thread and a leather needle with a triangular point. Wear a thimble to protect your finger.

Sweet william bag

MATERIALS REQUIRED

- 70 x 50cm (27⁵/₈ x 20in) taupe oilcloth with pink and red flowers
- 35 x 70cm (13³/₄ x 27⁵/₈in) maroon coated fabric
- 21 x 18cm (8¹/₄ x 7¹/₈in) coated linen fabric
- Pencil
- Needle
- Sewing thread in linen and maroon
- Translucent rocaille beads in red and pink
- Rocaille beads in matte white
- All-purpose scissors
- Pinking shears
- 40cm (16in) ruler
- Set square
- Tape measure
- Iron
- White cotton cloth
- Sewing machine

1. PREPARATION

Lay the floral-patterned oilcloth wrong side up and, using the diagram as a guide, draw out the pattern for the main section of the bag in pencil.

Lay the maroon coated fabric out wrong side up. Using a ruler and set square, mark out two strips 64 x 9cm (25¹/₄ x 3¹/₂in) and two strips 64 x 7cm (25¹/₄ x 2³/₄in).

Lastly, lay the coated linen wrong side up and, again using a ruler and set square, draw out three strips 2.5 x 18cm (1 x 7¹/₈in) and another three strips 1.5 x 18cm (³/₄ x 7¹/₈in).

Cut out the oilcloth bag section and the four strips of coated fabric using all-purpose scissors. Cut out the six strips of coated linen with pinking shears.

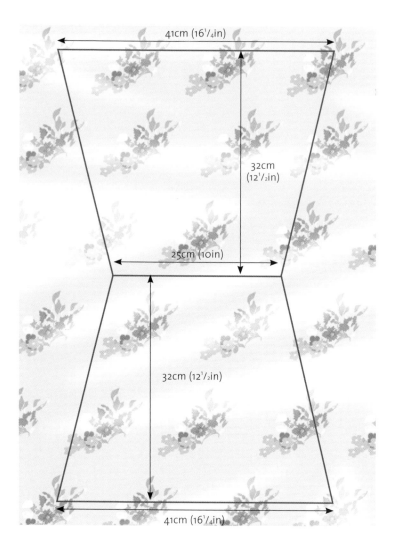

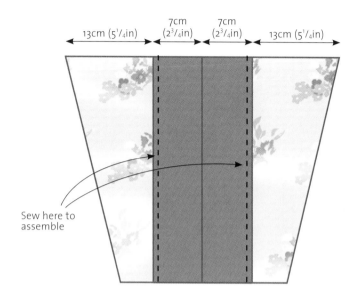

13cm (5¼in) 7cm (2¾in) 7cm (2¾in) 13cm (5¼in)

Sew here to assemble

4. SHAPING THE BAG BOTTOM

To make the bottom of the bag, flatten out the sides so that the seams are placed over the fold in the bottom of the bag to make a triangle 2cm (⅞in) high and with a 4cm (1⅝in) base. Use a pencil to draw the 4cm (1⅝in) lines and machine-sew along them. Refer to the diagram for the Sleepover bag on page 44 if necessary. Leave the bag wrong side out.

2. SEWING THE BAG TOGETHER

Take the two 64 x 9cm (25¼ x 3½in) strips of maroon coated fabric and fold 1cm (½in) to the wrong side along the two long edges. Press the two folds with an iron, placing a clean white cloth between the coated fabric and the iron. Machine-sew the two sides using maroon thread. Place the floral-patterned oilcloth right side up and position the two maroon strips either side of the centre line. There should be 13cm (5¼in) oilcloth on each side at the top. Pin and sew the outer edges of the two strips by machine, as shown in the diagram. As you sew, pull gently on the fabric to prevent puckering, as a presser foot has a tendency to stick to the fabric when working on the right side.

3. BAG ASSEMBLY

Once you have sewn on the two maroon strips, fold the oilcloth in half, right sides together. Using a ruler and pencil, draw a line on the reverse 1cm (½in) from the edge along the two sides.

These lines will show you where to sew. Pin and machine-sew the sides using maroon thread. Press the seams open with the point of an iron, placing a clean white cloth between the iron and the oilcloth.

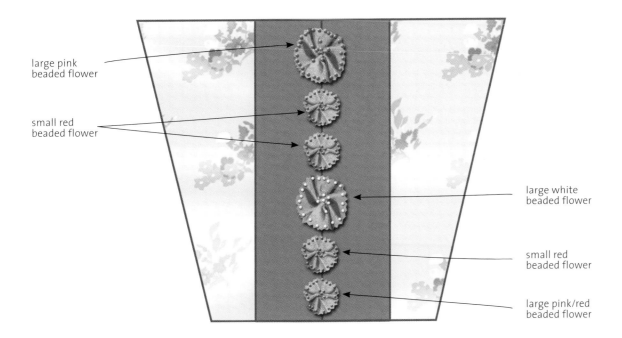

large pink
beaded flower

small red
beaded flower

large white
beaded flower

small red
beaded flower

large pink/red
beaded flower

5. MAKING THE HANDLES

Take the two remaining strips of maroon coated fabric and turn 1cm ('/₂in) to the wrong side along the two long edges. Press the fold with an iron.

Fold the strip in half lengthways, wrong sides together, pin and machine-sew using maroon thread. Sew a second row of stitches down the opposite side to match.

6. SEWING ON THE HANDLES

Turn 1cm ('/₂in) to the wrong side all round the top of the bag and pin. Position the handles inside the bag 10cm (4in) from the side seams and pin. Sew all the way around the top of the bag and over the handles using maroon thread. Turn the bag right side out.

7. MAKING THE SWEET WILLIAMS

Sew a very wide running stitch (see page 15) along one long edge of each strip of coated linen in matching thread. When you reach the end, gently pull the thread to gather the strip into a round. Secure the circle you have made by sewing the two ends together tightly.

8. DECORATING THE SWEET WILLIAMS

Sew a rocaille bead on to each point made by the pinking shears. Sew several beads into the centre, too. Make up three large flowers as follows: one pink beaded flower, one white beaded flower and one red and pink beaded flower. Sew red beads on to the three small flowers. You now have six flowers.

9. SEWING THE FLOWERS TO THE BAG

Attach the flowers to the inside edges of your maroon coated fabric strips, which are not sewn down. Distribute the stitches evenly over the two strips. Refer to the diagram for help with the positioning of the flowers.

SUMMER ESSENTIALS

Picnic pouffe

MATERIALS REQUIRED

- Round of dense foam 8cm (3^1/$_4$in) thick and 40cm (16in) in diameter
- 50 x 100cm (20 x 40in) thick oilcloth in pink with white polka dots + one strip 16 x 7cm (6^1/$_2$ x 2^3/$_4$in) for the flowers on the strap
- 20 x 140cm (8 x 55in) thick oilcloth in red with white polka dots + one strip 26 x 13cm (10^1/$_4$ x 5^1/$_4$in) for the strap
- Thick leather needle with triangular point
- Nylon thread 2^1/$_2$mm thick
- Pins
- Thimble
- Hole punch
- Cyanoacrylate-based superglue
- Double-sided tape
- 40cm (16in) metal ruler
- Soft pencil
- Tracing paper
- Pair of compasses
- All-purpose scissors

1. CUTTING OUT THE PIECES

On the back of the pink oilcloth, draw two circles 43cm (17in) in diameter using a pair of compasses.
Cut them out carefully.
Lay the long strip of red oilcloth wrong side up and draw a strip 9^1/$_2$ x 140cm (3^3/$_4$ x 55in) with your pencil, making sure that the lines are absolutely straight and parallel.
Cut it out. On the wrong side of the small strip of red oilcloth, draw two 13 x 6cm (5^1/$_4$ x 2^1/$_2$in) rectangles. Cut them out.

2. PUTTING THE POUFFE TOGETHER

Lay one pink oilcloth circle wrong side up and, with wrong sides together, pin one edge of the long strip of red oilcloth all the way round.
Pin at approximately 2cm (^{7}/$_8$in) intervals and overlap the ends of the red strip by 2^1/$_2$cm (1in), trimming any excess.

3. SEWING THE POUFFE

Thread the thick leather needle with 30cm (12in) length of nylon thread. Do not use too long a thread because nylon thread has an unfortunate tendency to tangle, which will disrupt your work. Sew the pink circle to the red strip using a blanket stitch over the edges (see page 15).
The stitches should be about 4mm (^{1}/$_4$in) tall, spaced every 3mm (^{1}/$_8$in) apart. When you have been all the way around the pouffe, finish by sewing the two ends of the red strip together with a backstitch (see page 15). Insert the foam pad. Take the second pink circle, pin it to the red strip as you did the first circle and sew round it using blanket stitch as before.

4. MAKING THE STRAP

Take the two small 13 x 6cm (5¼ x 2½in) strips of red oilcloth that you have cut out. On the wrong side of one of the pieces, stick two 10cm (4in) lengths of double-sided tape along the centre. Stick the two strips together, wrong sides together. Attach this strap to the pouffe over the join in the red strip.

Sew the top of the strap on to the pouffe with a double row of backstitch (see page 15). Sew the bottom of the strap on to the edge with the blanket stitch, not under the pouffe, using backstitch again.

5. MAKING THE FLOWERS AND THE SPOTS

Copy the flower template on to tracing paper and cut it out. Lay the offcuts of pink oilcloth wrong sides up and copy the outline of the flower three times, centering them around a white polka dot each time. Cut them out. Using a hole punch, punch three red mini dots from a scrap of red oilcloth. Glue one to the centre of each flower. Now glue the three flowers on to the strap. Using the same technique, make seven red flowers from offcuts of red oilcloth. Glue them on to the pouffe. Using a hole punch, punch about 32 small red dots and glue these round the white polka dots. You will need about eight small dots to make each small flower.

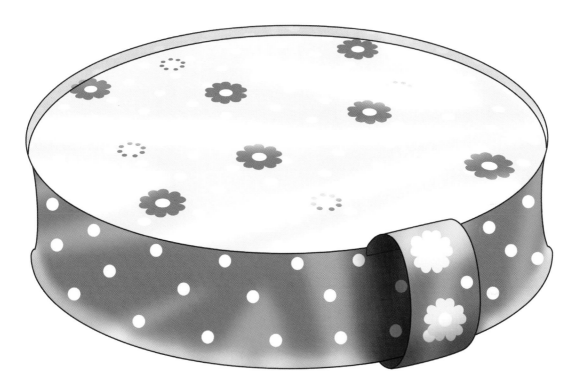

Butterfly tea caddy

MATERIALS REQUIRED

- Rectangular tea caddy
- 53 x 12cm (21 x 4³/₄in) raspberry oilcloth
- 10cm (4in) square oilcloth with butterfly print
- Brass label holder
- Cotton wool ball
- Sheet pink paper
- Fine leather needle with triangular point
- Invisible nylon thread
- Silver-coated copper wire 2.8mm in diameter
- Pins
- Superglue
- PVA adhesive
- Synthetic paintbrush
- Double-sided tape
- Pencil
- Tracing paper
- Cutting mat
- Rotary cutter
- Flat metal ruler
- All-purpose scissors

1. PREPARATION

Using a rotary cutter, cut a strip of raspberry oilcloth 8.3 x 39cm (3¹/₄ x 15¹/₂in), ensuring that the angles are perfectly square. Place the tracing paper on the lid of the caddy and draw around the outline in pencil. Cut it out. Place the template on the wrong side of the remaining oilcloth and copy the outline. Cut it out.

Cut two large butterflies and two smaller butterflies from the butterfly print oilcloth.

2. MAKING THE LARGE BUTTERFLY

Place one large butterfly wrong side up and attach a small piece of double-sided tape across each pair of wings, at right angles to the body. Cut two lengths of copper wire slightly shorter than the tape. Place one length of copper wire on each piece of tape. Cover the butterfly with a small amount of cotton wool. Place the second butterfly on top of the first, wrong sides together. Sew them together round the edge with a small running stitch (see page 15) using nylon thread.

3. MAKING THE SLEEVE

Wrap the strip of raspberry oilcloth around your tea caddy. Insert a pin to mark the join. Remove the strip and with right sides together sew the ends together with a very narrow double row of backstitch (see page 15) on the reverse. Trim the excess oilcloth. Slide the sleeve into position on the caddy.

4. FINISHING OFF

Using a paintbrush, coat the piece of oilcloth for the lid with PVA adhesive. Stick it on to the lid and smooth out gently. Leave to dry for at least one hour. Cut a label from pink paper and slide it into the label holder. Apply a few spots of superglue to the label holder and stick it on to the front of the caddy.

Using superglue, attach the two small butterflies to the front of the caddy. To stick down the large butterfly to the centre of the lid apply glue to the body but not the wings and position it. When the glue has dried, bend the reinforced wings of the large butterfly up slightly.

Personal sketchbook

MATERIALS REQUIRED

(for a 27cm (10½in) square sketchbook)

- 90 x 35cm (35½ x 13¾in) thick oilcloth in green with large multicoloured flowers
- Ruler
- All-purpose scissors
- Stuffing
- 1 self-adhesive Velcro circle 1cm (½in) diameter
- Fine leather needle with triangular point
- Invisible polyamide thread
- Superglue
- 2 large and 3 small translucent green flower-shaped buttons
- Double-sided tape
- Iron and white cotton cloth

1. PREPARING YOUR MATERIALS

Cut out a 77 x 27.8cm (30¼ x 11in) rectangle from the oilcloth for the cover and a strip 28 x 4cm (11 x 1⅝in) for the strap. Cut two flowers about 6cm (2½in) in diameter from the offcuts.

2. MAKING THE COVER

Fold 10cm (4in) to the wrong side on the two short sides of the oilcloth rectangle. Press the folds with a cool iron, placing a clean cloth between the iron and the oilcloth. With a leather needle and polyamide thread, sew along the right side of the flaps 3mm (⅛in) from the edge, at the top and bottom, using a small running stitch (see page 15). Try the cover on for size and then take the sketchbook out.

3. MAKING THE STRAP AND FLOWER

Fold the 28 x 4cm (11 x 1⅝in) strip of oilcloth in half lengthways. Hold together with a few pieces of double-sided tape. Using invisible thread, sew a running stitch all the way around the strap 2mm (⅛in) from the edge. Place the two cut-out oilcloth flowers wrong sides together and sew round the edge using a running stitch. Stop before the last petal and stuff the flower before sewing it up. Glue the flower on to the end of the strap. Glue one half of the Velcro circle on to the underside of the strap under the flower.

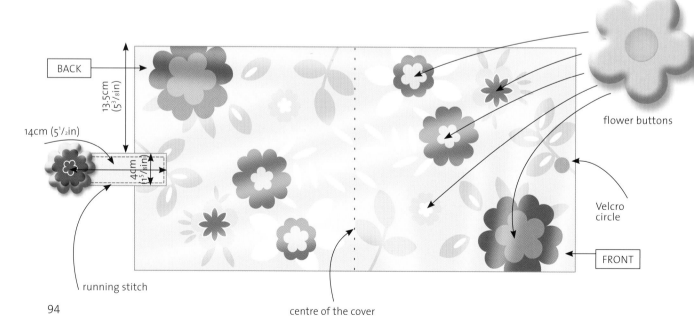

BACK

13.5cm (5⅜in)

14cm (5½in)

4cm (1⅝in)

running stitch

flower buttons

Velcro circle

FRONT

centre of the cover

4. ATTACHING THE STRAP TO THE COVER

Position the strap 13.5cm (5³/₈in) from the top edge on the back of the cover. Using polyamide thread, sew the strap to the cover with running stitch over the top of the first stitches, going back through the holes already made. Be careful not to sew through the flap too!

5. FINISHING TOUCHES

Place the sketchbook back in its cover and close the clasp. Mark where the second half of the Velcro circle should go and attach. On the front of the cover, glue the flower-shaped buttons into the centre of the flowers printed on the oilcloth.

Babushka table runner

MATERIALS REQUIRED

- 50 x 25cm (20 x 10in) taupe oilcloth with red and pink flowers
- 35 x 10cm (13$^3/_4$ x 4in) cherry-red oilcloth
- 40 x 140cm (16 x 55in) raspberry oilcloth
- 45 x 140cm (17$^3/_4$ x 55in) linen-coloured coated linen
- 33 x 11cm (13 x 4$^3/_8$in) coated damask in almond green
- 27 x 9cm (10$^1/_2$ x 3$^1/_2$in) coated damask in maroon
- 24 x 8cm (9$^1/_2$ x 3$^1/_4$in) coated damask in beige
- Black fine 0.1 felt-tip pen
- 3 sheets tracing paper
- Pencil
- Superglue
- Invisible polyamide thread
- Needle
- All-purpose scissors
- Embroidery scissors
- 40cm (16in) ruler
- Set square
- Tape measure
- Iron
- White cloth

1. MAKING THE TEMPLATES

Copy all the templates for the doll given on page 97 on to tracing paper. For the braiding, trace the design and cut out the pattern.

2. PREPARING AND CUTTING OUT THE BASE

Lay the rectangle of linen-coloured coated fabric wrong side up. Iron with a clean white cloth. When the fabric is smooth and has cooled down, cut out a rectangle 140 x 40cm (55 x 16in). Shop-cut material rarely has straight edges so ensure that yours are at perfect right angles.

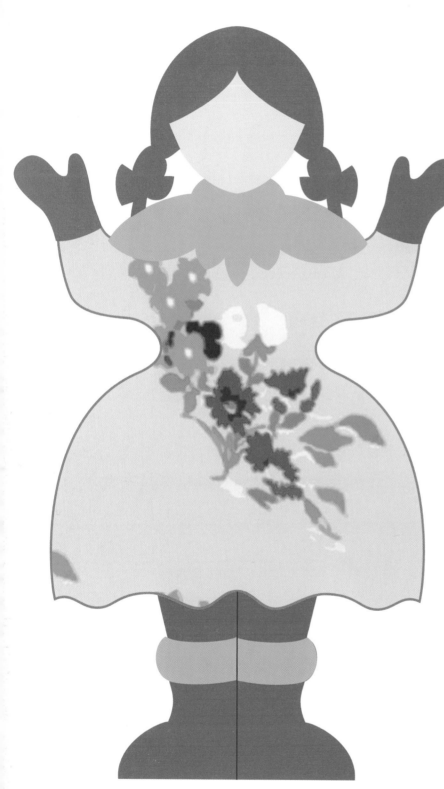

3. PREPARING AND CUTTING OUT THE BRAIDING

Place the rectangle of raspberry oilcloth wrong side up. If it is creased or has small cracks, iron it on the reverse, placing a clean white cloth under the iron. When the oilcloth is smooth, cut three strips 140 x 4cm (55 x 1⅝in) wide. Take the first strip and place the braid template you have cut out on the wrong side of the oilcloth.

Copy the outline, moving the template along as you go. Repeat this process on the second strip. On the third strip, mark out only 90cm (35½in) of braiding. Cut out all the strips carefully with embroidery scissors. If your scissors are too large you will have problems cutting the curved sections – and there are lots of them!

4. PREPARING AND CUTTING OUT THE HEARTS

To make the four large hearts, enlarge the template by 20 per cent and transfer it on to the wrong side of the raspberry oilcloth. Cut the hearts out with embroidery scissors. Trace the small heart using the same technique and copy it to give you 18 small hearts in the floral oilcloth and 9 small hearts in the raspberry oilcloth.

5. MAKING UP THE DOLLS

Take all the oilcloth pieces corresponding to the different parts of the doll and lay each piece wrong side up. Use the tracing paper to copy the motifs on to the oilcloths and cut them out using embroidery scissors. Thread a needle with 25cm (10in) invisible polyamide thread and sew each doll together as follows: sew the right mitten under the sleeve of the dress and, without tying off or starting a new thread, move straight to the green scarf over the dress and finish with the left mitten under the sleeve. Sew the hair over the face and the face over the green scarf. Finally sew the borders on to the boots and the boots under the dress.

6. FINAL ASSEMBLY

Take the linen-coloured coated fabric cloth and lay it right side up. Using the photo and the diagram as a guide, start to add all the pieces until the dolls are perfectly aligned and the overall composition is to your taste. Glue each item by lifting each one, taking care not to move them. Use the glue sparingly. Keep a white cloth to hand to wipe off marks as soon as they appear.

140cm (55in)

4.5cm (1¹⁄₂in) 15.5cm (6¹⁄₄in) 23cm (9in) 15.5cm (6¹⁄₄in) 23cm (9i

15.5cm (6¼in)   23cm (9in)   15.5cm (6¼in)   4.5cm (1½in)

40cm (16in)

Large shopper

MATERIALS REQUIRED

- 119 x 50cm (47 x 20in) thick oilcloth in sky blue with small red and white flowers
- 55 x 40cm (21³/₄ x 16in) thick oilcloth in sky blue with red, pink and white stripes
- Fine leather needle with triangular point
- Needle
- Sewing machine
- White sewing thread
- Sewing thread in sky blue to match the oilcloth
- Nylon thread 3.5mm in diameter
- All-purpose scissors
- Double-sided tape
- Iron
- White cotton cloth
- Tracing paper
- 1 small red eyelet
- Tape measure
- Long ruler
- Set square
- Pencil
- 20cm (8in) pink leather thonging
- Stuffing
- Keyring

1. PREPARATION

Lay the piece of floral oilcloth wrong side up and, with the aid of a ruler and set square, mark out two 52 x 25cm (20¹/₂ x 10in) pieces and two strips 10 x 67cm (4 x 26³/₈in) for the two handles.

On the back of the striped oilcloth, and again using your ruler and set square, draw a rectangle 37 x 52cm (14⁵/₈ x 20¹/₂in) wide with the stripes running lengthways. Refer to the diagram if necessary. Cut out all the pieces.

2. SEWING TOGETHER YOUR THREE PIECES OF OILCLOTH

Place a rectangle of floral oilcloth along one of the long edges of your striped oilcloth, with right sides together, and pin. Draw a line on the reverse 1cm (¹/₂in) from the edge and machine-sew using white thread. Sew the second rectangle of floral oilcloth along the other long edge of the striped oilcloth in the same way.

87cm (34¹/₄in)

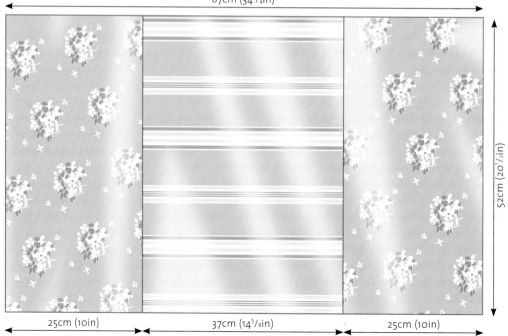

52cm (20¹/₂in)

25cm (10in) 37cm (14⁵/₈in) 25cm (10in)

61cm
(24in)

10cm (4in)

10cm (4in)

21cm (8¹⁄₄in)

11cm (4³⁄₈in)

49cm (19¹⁄₄in)

4. SHAPING THE BOTTOM OF THE BAG

To shape the bottom of the bag, flatten the side seams and place them over the fold in the bottom of the bag to make a triangle 5cm (2in) high and with a 10cm (4in) base. Using your pencil, mark the 10cm (4in) lines and machine-sew. Refer to the diagram for the Sleepover bag on page 44 if necessary.

5. SEWING THE HANDLES

Lay the two 67 x 10cm (26³⁄₈ x 4in) strips wrong side up. Fold 1cm (¹⁄₂in), over to the wrong side, along both long edges. Press these folds with your nail, then fold each strip in half to give you strips 4cm (1⁵⁄₈in) wide. Secure the folded strips with paper clips and machine-sew 5mm (¹⁄₄in) from the edge, using sky blue thread and removing the paper clips as you go. Sew a second row on the other side, 5mm (¹⁄₄in) from the edge.

3. BAG ASSEMBLY

Set the iron to between the wool and cotton settings and, placing a clean white cloth between the iron and the oilcloth, open and flatten out the seams with the tip of your iron, on the wrong side. While the seams are still warm and supple, cut 8cm (3¹⁄₄in) lengths of double-sided tape and stick them along the two seams so they stay flat. Fold the three joined pieces in half, right sides together and matching the seams. Draw a line 1.5cm (³⁄₄in) from the edge along the right and left sides and pin. Machine-sew the two sides. When you reach the joins between the different oilcloths you will be sewing through four layers. Help the machine by pulling the oilcloth gently towards you. Take your time, or you risk breaking the needle. Press the seams open with the iron over a cloth.

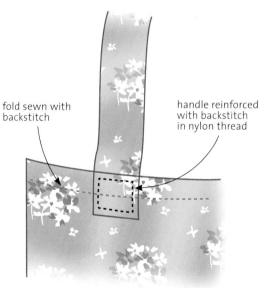

fold sewn with backstitch

handle reinforced with backstitch in nylon thread

7. MAKING AND ATTACHING THE HEART

Copy the heart template on to tracing paper and cut it out. Copy the outline twice on to the wrong side of the striped oilcloth. Cut out and sew together all round with blanket stitch (see page 15) starting at the centre of the top. Just before you reach the end, stuff the heart, then finish the blanket stitching and finally sew on the small ring of the keyring. Add an eyelet to the top edge of the bag, thread the leather thonging through it, pass it through the large ring of the keyring and go back through the eyelet. Knot the leather thonging inside the bag.

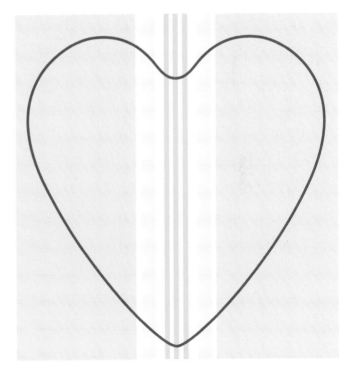

6. SEWING THE HANDLES TO THE BAG

Fold the top edge of the bag 3cm (1¼in) to the wrong side and secure with paper clips.

Place the handles on either side, pinning them 10cm (4in) from the side seams. Backstitch (see page 15) all the way around approximately 1.5cm (¾in) from the edge. This will secure the handles at the same time as the inside flap. Because large shoppers often have to carry heavy loads, reinforce the stitching around the handle by backstitching in invisible nylon thread on the four sides.

Café tablecloth

MATERIALS REQUIRED

(for a table 68 x 44cm (26³/₄ x 17³/₈in))

- 76cm (30in) square of white oilcloth with a vivid red pattern
- 160 x 90cm (63 x 35¹/₂in) white coated fabric
- 5.3m (6yd) bias binding in vivid red
- Vivid red sewing thread
- White sewing thread
- Ruler
- Pencil
- All-purpose scissors
- 18 flower-shaped fuchsia mother-of-pearl buttons 2cm (⁷/₈in) in diameter
- Pins
- Needle
- Fine leather needle with triangular point
- Iron and white cotton cloth

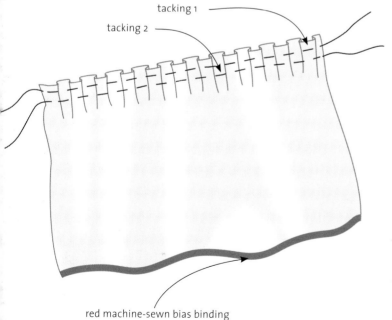

tacking 1

tacking 2

red machine-sewn bias binding

BEFORE YOU START

This design was made for a low table measuring 68 x 44cm (26³/₄ x 17³/₈in). To work out the amount of oilcloth and coated fabric needed to adapt the design to fit another table, measure the table top and add 1.5cm (³/₄in) to each side. If your table is 68cm (26³/₄in) wide, you would need 68cm + 1.5cm + 1.5cm: a total of 71cm (26³/₄in + ³/₄in + ³/₄in: a total of 28¹/₄in), to which you should add 5cm (2in) for security. This will tell you how much oilcloth to purchase. For the coated fabric skirt, simply double the length and width of the table.

1. MAKING THE FLOUNCES

Place the coated fabric wrong side up and, with a ruler and pencil, draw two strips 155 x 20cm (61 x 8in) for the long edges and two strips 110 x 20cm (43¹/₄ x 8in) for the widths. Cut out the strips and iron.

Attach bias binding to the long edge of each strip, sewing it on the right side so it sits on top, using red thread. Thread a needle with a generous length of white thread and sew a fairly long running stitch (see page 15) about 3mm (¹/₈in) from the top edge of one long strip, the opposite side from the bias binding, leaving a long end of thread at the start and the end. Just below this line, sew a second line of running stitch in the same way. Gather the coated fabric by pulling on the right and left ends and spread the pleats out evenly. Use the diagram as a guide. Check that the length of the long flounce is the same length as the table before tying the threads together at the sides to secure the flounce. Repeat for the three other strips, checking the lengths against the top sides of the table.Join the four flounces by placing the ends right sides together and alternating short and long strips. Pin and machine-sew on the reverse using white thread.

2. ATTACHING THE SKIRT TO THE TABLECLOTH

Draw a rectangle 71 x 47cm (28 x 18½in) on the back of the oilcloth and cut out. This is the top of your tablecloth. Lay the rectangle right side up. Put the flouncing on top, right sides together, and line up the side seams with the corners. Pin at regular intervals and tack all round using white sewing thread. Use the diagram as a guide if necessary. Machine-sew on the reverse. Once the flounce is attached, iron the pleats with a cool iron one last time. Remember to place a cloth between the iron and the oilcloth.

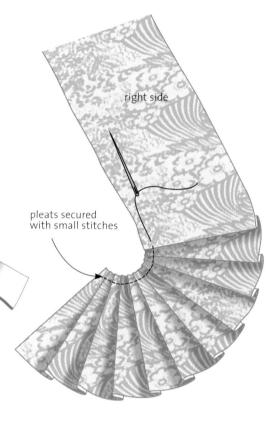

right side

pleats secured
with small stitches

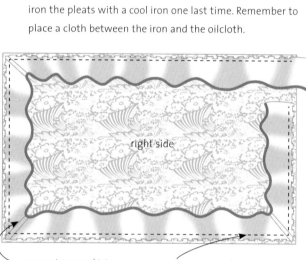

right side

seam to sew skirt
together

seam to sew skirt to
tablecloth

3. MAKING THE ROSETTES

In the remaining oilcloth, draw 18 strips 3 x 35cm (1¼ x 13¾in) and cut them out. Take a strip and start to make pleats, sewing them as you work using a triangular-pointed leather needle and white thread. When you have made up all the flowers, sew a mother-of-pearl button in the centre of each one.

4. ADDING THE ROSETTES

Pin the rosettes evenly over the flounce. Attach them by passing your needle through the holes in the mother-of-pearl buttons. Be careful not to sew through the pleats.

right side with
skirt turned over

Padded child's chair

MATERIALS REQUIRED

- 1 padded child's chair
- 50cm (20in) square white oilcloth with brightly-coloured flower pattern
- 70 x 20cm (27⅝ x 8in) white coated fabric
- 4m (4½yd) poppy-red bias binding
- Red sewing thread to match the bias binding
- White sewing thread
- Sewing machine
- All-purpose scissors
- 40cm (16in) ruler
- Tape measure
- Pencil
- Needle

1. PREPARING AND CUTTING OUT THE SEAT

Start by enlarging the seat template by 260 per cent. Cut the template out on paper. Place the paper template on the square of floral oilcloth laid wrong side up and copy it, drawing all the lines with a ruler. Cut out the seat. If the style of your chair is very different, make a template of the seat with tissue paper, adding about 3–4cm (1¼–1⅝in) extra all the way around the chair. Continue to follow the instructions.

SEAT
template

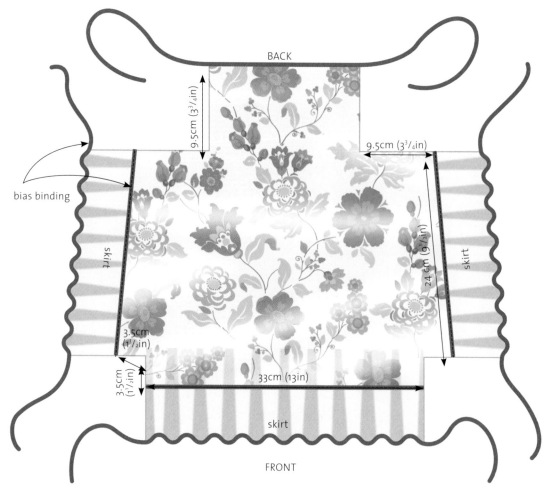

BACK

9.5cm (3³/₄in)

9.5cm (3³/₄in)

bias binding

skirt

skirt

24 cm (9¹/₂in)

3.5cm (1¹/₂in)

3.5cm (1¹/₂in)

33cm (13in)

skirt

FRONT

2. PREPARING THE SKIRT

Cut one 60 x 6.5cm (23¹/₂ x 2⁵/₈in) piece and two 50 x 6.5cm (20 x 2⁵/₈in) pieces from the rectangle of white coated fabric. Cut two 1m (40in) lengths and one 1.2m (48in) length from the bias binding. Attach the bias binding to each skirt by sewing it on the right side so it sits over the coated fabric, using red thread and leaving 25cm (10in) excess binding at each end. Thread a needle with a generous amount of white thread. Work a fairly long running stitch (see page 15) on the reverse along the side opposite the bias binding and about 3mm (¹/₈in) from the edge, leaving a long end of thread at the start and end.

Just below this line, sew a second row of running stitches in the same way. Gather the coated fabric by pulling on the threads at each end and even out the gathers. Repeat these steps for the other two strips of white coated fabric.

3. ADAPTING THE SKIRT TO THE SEAT

Take the oilcloth seat and adjust the gathers on the lengths of the skirts to fit. When they are the right size, tie the two threads together at each end to secure them.

1- Sew a running stitch, leaving a generous length of thread at the start and end

2- Pull to gather

4. ATTACHING THE SKIRT TO THE SEAT

Lay the oilcloth seat right side up and place the skirt pieces on top, right sides facing, and line up the edges. Refer to the diagram if necessary. Tack all the way around. This is an essential step before sewing the skirt by machine using white thread. When you have sewn on the three skirts, turn them to the right side.

5. FINISHING TOUCHES

Cut three new lengths of red bias binding as follows: 1 x 33cm (13in) and 2 x 24cm (9½in). Sew bias binding over the white stitching joining the skirt to the seat, to hide it. This will give a neat finish, and sewing over the stitching will stop the skirt from rising up. This last step can be a difficult procedure because of the number of layers you are dealing with. Work slowly to prevent your sewing machine grinding to a halt. Ease the oilcloth through the machine by pulling gently as you sew.

Finish by attaching the bias binding to the back of the seat, leaving 25cm (10in) excess on both sides.

3- Place the skirt on the seat right sides together

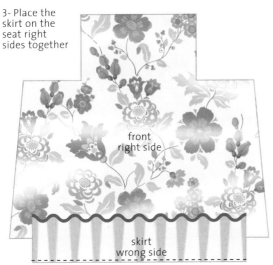

4- Turn out

113

Pretty-as-a-picture clogs

MATERIALS REQUIRED

- 1 pair brightly-coloured patent leather clogs
- 80 x 14cm (31$\frac{1}{2}$ x 5$\frac{1}{2}$in) thick oilcloth with a flower print
- Large rocaille beads in mauve
- Small flower-shaped hole punch
- Fine leather needle with triangular point
- Invisible polyamide thread
- Superglue
- Pencil
- Tracing paper
- Small all-purpose scissors

1. PREPARING THE FLOWERS

Copy the two flowers on to tracing paper and cut them out carefully. Cut two 12cm (4$\frac{3}{4}$in) squares and six 9cm (3$\frac{1}{2}$in) squares from the oilcloth. Place these squares on the table wrong side up and copy the outline of the large flower on to the two 12cm (4$\frac{3}{4}$in) squares and the outline of the small flower on to the six 9cm (3$\frac{1}{2}$in) squares using a pencil. Cut out all the flowers.

2. MAKING THE FLOWERS

Thread a leather needle with a 30cm (12in) length of thread. Tie several knots in the end. Take a small flower and, with the wrong side facing you, fold one petal towards the centre so that the right side can be seen, and attach it to the centre of the flower with a few stitches. Repeat this process for all the petals. Sew three mauve beads into the centre of the flower. Using scissors, make three or four 1cm ($\frac{1}{2}$in) slits in the fold of each petal. Do not make the slits too long or you may cut into the stitching that attaches the end of the petal to the centre. Make up four small flowers in this way. To make the two double flowers, glue or sew one small flower on to one large flower, then add the beads at the end.

3. FINISHING OFF AND ASSEMBLY

Superglue one double flower and two small flowers on to the outer side of each clog. Using a punch, make twelve mini flowers from offcuts of the oilcloth and sew a bead into the centre of each. Glue the flowers on to the upper strap of your clogs with superglue.

Child's apron

MATERIALS REQUIRED

- 60 x 48cm (23$\frac{1}{2}$ x 19in) thick oilcloth in red with white polka dots
- 30 x 20cm (12 x 8in) thick oilcloth in pink with white polka dots
- 12cm (4$\frac{3}{4}$in) square oilcloth with small flower motif
- 4cm (1$\frac{5}{8}$in) square oilcloth in raspberry
- 110 x 3cm (43$\frac{1}{4}$ x 1$\frac{1}{4}$in) coated gingham in ecru
- 10 x 3cm (4 x 1$\frac{1}{4}$in) coated gingham in ecru
- 3.05m (120$\frac{1}{8}$in) bias binding in pink with white polka dots
- Sewing needle
- Sewing thread in ecru and pale pink
- Pins
- Adhesive putty
- Double-sided tape 3mm ($\frac{1}{8}$in) wide
- Sticky tape
- Cyanoacrylate-based superglue
- Sheet brown wrapping paper 60 x 50cm (23$\frac{1}{2}$ x 20in)
- Pencil
- Sewing machine
- 40cm (16in) ruler
- Tape measure
- All-purpose scissors
- Iron
- Clean white tea towel

1. MAKING UP THE TEMPLATES

Enlarge the patterns for the apron and the pocket by 370 per cent, then photocopy the various motifs that make up the cake to go on the pocket. Cut out all the templates carefully.

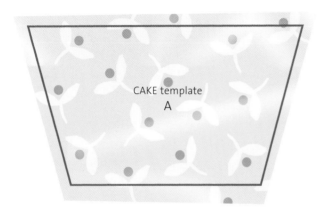

CAKE template
A

CAKE template
B

2. CUTTING OUT THE PIECES

Lay the red oilcloth wrong side up and place the paper pattern of the apron you have cut out on top and hold in place with a little adhesive putty at the top, bottom and sides. Smooth the pattern out so it lies perfectly flat on the oilcloth.

Using a pencil, copy the outline, marking the straight lines with the aid of a ruler.

Use the same technique for the pink polka dot pocket. For the four motifs that make up the cake (cherry, cream, top and centre part), there is no need to stick the template down with adhesive putty. Simply hold the template with your hand while you draw around the motif. When you have copied all the templates, cut out the pieces carefully inside the lines.

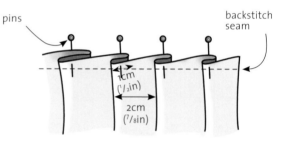

pins

backstitch seam

1cm ($^{1}/_{2}$in)

2cm ($^{7}/_{8}$in)

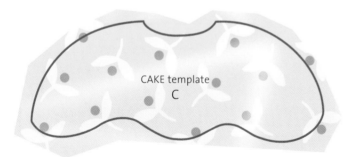

CAKE template
C

3. MAKING THE FRILL

Make the pocket frill from the 110 x 3cm (43$^{1}/_{4}$ x 1$^{1}/_{4}$in) strip of ecru coated fabric. Fold 1cm ($^{1}/_{2}$in) of the fabric over and pin the pleat at the top. Leave 2cm ($^{7}/_{8}$in), then fold 1cm ($^{1}/_{2}$in) of the oilcloth over again. Repeat until the whole strip is pleated. To mark the folds, iron the back of the strip on the cotton setting, placing a clean tea towel between the iron and the frill. Using ecru sewing thread, secure all the pleats with a small backstitch (see page 15) 3mm ($^{1}/_{8}$in) from the edge. Take the pins out as you go.

CAKE template
D

4. SEWING ON THE FLOUNCE

Cut four 2.5cm (1in) lengths of double-sided tape. Place them evenly over the length of the pleated frill, sticking them about 2mm ($^1/_8$in) from the upper edge. Take the pink polka dot pocket and, using pins, secure the frill under the curved edge, about 5mm ($^1/_4$in) underneath. The visible frill should be about 2.5cm (1in) wide. Using pale pink thread, sew the frill to the pocket with a running stitch (see page 15) close to the edge of the pocket.

5. ADDING THE MOTIF

Apply a little glue to the backs of the four sections that make up the cake. Glue them one at a time to the pocket, starting from the bottom, in the following order: A, B, C, D, as shown in the diagram below. Leave out flat to dry for one hour.

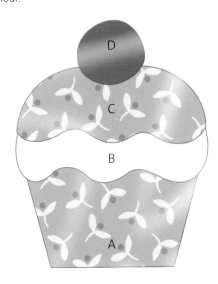

6. SEWING THE POCKET TO THE APRON

Machine-sew a 27cm (10$^3/_8$in) length of bias binding to the top of the pocket using pale pink thread. Position the pocket in the centre of the apron, 6cm (2$^1/_2$in) from the bottom. Hold in place with a few pieces of tape that you can remove as you work to prevent the pocket from sliding around as you sew. Machine-sew with pink thread.

7. ADDING THE BIAS BINDING TO THE TOP OF THE APRON

Machine-sew 17cm (6$^3/_4$in) of bias binding to the top of the apron using pale pink thread. Take the remaining length of bias binding, fold it in half lengthways and iron to mark the fold. Make a 50cm (20in) loop above the top edge of the apron and then pin down the sides to secure. Leave the ends of the binding on both sides to tie the apron. Machine-sew using pale pink thread.

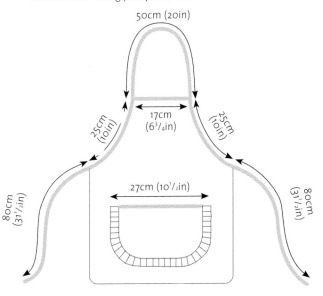

THE DESIGNS

THE GREAT OUTDOORS

Princess wellingtons

(page 18)

Flower coasters

(page 20)

Mini armchair

(page 22)

Vanity case

(page 28)

Butterfly doilies

(page 26)

My outdoor jacket
(page 32)

Child's picnic tablecloth
(page 36)

Floral apron
(page 40)

Sleepover bag
(page 44)

VINTAGE CHIC

Gingham storage jar
(page 50)

Recipe notebook
(page 52)

Jam jar hats
(page 54)

Wicker shopping
basket (page 58)

Elegant flowerpot
holder (page 62)

Camellia bag
(page 66)

Exotic place mats
(page 70)

Toile de jouy dishes
(page 74)

Daffodil vase
(page 76)

English country
tablecloth (page 78)

Sweet william bag
(page 82)

SUMMER ESSENTIALS

Picnic pouffe
(page 88)

Butterfly tea caddy
(page 92)

Personal sketchbook
(page 94)

Babushka table runner
(page 96)

Large shopper
(page 102)

Café tablecloth
(page 106)

Padded child's chair
(page 110)

Pretty-as-a-picture
clogs (page 114)

Child's apron
(page 116)

USEFUL ADDRESSES

OILCLOTH SUPPLIERS

UK

CATH KIDSTON
www.cathkidston.co.uk
08450 262 440

OILCLOTH UK
Stocks a range of Mexican Oilcloth, as well
as providing useful general information.
www.oilcloth.co.uk
oilcloth@hotmail.co.uk

TREEHOUSE BLUE
Small selection of oilcloth available by the metre.
www.treehouseblue.co.uk

C&H
Online store, as well as retail outlets in the UK.
www.candh.co.uk
01892 773600

US

MENDEL'S FAR-OUT FABRIC
1556 Haight Street
San Francisco, CA 94117
Online store and retail shop selling
oilcloth by the yard or roll.
www.mendels.com
(415) 621-1287

FABRICS.NET
Online store selling oilcloth by the roll.
www.fabrics.net
(800) 483-5598

GENERAL CRAFT AND FABRIC SUPPLIERS

UK

CARNMEAL COTTAGE
Carnmeal Downs
Breage, Helston
Cornwall, TR13 9NL
Retail and wholesale craft supplies
www.carnmeal.com

FABRICLAND
Fabric Towers, Kingfisher Park
Headland, Salisbury Road Ringwood, BH24 3NX
Retail dress and craft fabrics, haberdashery and trimmings
www.fabricland.co.uk

GROVES AND BANK
Drakes Drive Industrial Estate
Long Crendon, Aylesbury
HP18 9BA
Wholesale haberdashery
www.groves-banks.com

HABICO
Tong Road Industrial Estate
Amberley Road
Leeds, LS12 4BD
Wholesale haberdashery, trimmings, Bondaweb
www.habico.co.uk

JOHN LEWIS
Draycott Avenue,
London, SW3 2NA
Retail craft, dress and furnishing fabric, and haberdashery
www.johnlewis.com

KLEINS
5 Noel Street
London, W1F 8GD
Wholesale trimmings
www.kleins.co.uk

MORPLAN LTD
PO Box 54
Harlow
Essex
CM20 2TS
Retail and wholesale suppliers, pattern cutting equipment
www.morplan.com

US

BJ'S CRAFT SUPPLIES
203 Bickford Rd, Tivoli,
TX 77990-4546
General craft supplies, online store
www.bjcraftsupplies.com
(361) 286 3366

JO-ANN
5555 Darrow Rd.
Hudson, OH 44236
Fabric nd craft suppliers, online store
www.joann.com
(888) 739 4120

3 6058 00155 3862